How to Use This Book

Look for these special features in this book:

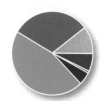

SIDEBARS, **CHARTS**, **GRAPHS**, and original **MAPS** expand your understanding of what's being discussed—and also make useful sources for classroom reports.

FAQs answer common **F**requently **A**sked **Q**uestions about people, places, and things.

WOW FACTORS offer "Who knew?" facts to keep you thinking.

TRAVEL GUIDE gives you tips on exploring the state—either in person or right from your chair!

PROJECT ROOM provides fun ideas for school assignments and incredible research projects. Plus, there's a guide to primary sources—what they are and how to cite them.

Please note: All statistics are as up-to-date as possible at the time of publication.

Consultants: Martha Coons, Young Adult Librarian, Springfield City Library; William Loren Katz; Joseph P. Kopera, Office of the Massachusetts State Geologist

Book production by The Design Lab

Library of Congress Cataloging-in-Publication Data
Trueit, Trudi Strain.
 Massachusetts / by Trudi Strain Trueit.
    p. cm.—(America, the beautiful. Third series)
Includes bibliographical references and index.
ISBN-13: 978-0-531-18561-2
ISBN-10: 0-531-18561-3
1. Massachusetts—Juvenile literature. I. Title. II. Series.
F64.3.T78 2008
974.4—dc22   2006039235

1 2 3 4 5 6 7 8 9 10 R 17 16 15 14 13 12 11 10 09 08

AMERICA ★ THE ★ BEAUTIFUL

Massachusetts

BY TRUDI STRAIN TRUEIT

Third Series

Children's Press®
A Division of Scholastic Inc.
New York ★ Toronto ★ London ★ Auckland ★ Sydney
Mexico City ★ New Delhi ★ Hong Kong
Danbury, Connecticut

CONTENTS

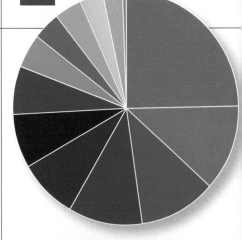

4

Daring inventors and waves of immigrants make the Bay State the heart of America's Industrial Revolution.. . . . . **46**

GROWTH AND CHANGE

MORE MODERN TIMES

5

The stock market crashes, technology comes of age, and dreams of space travel are born. . . . **56**

Robert Goddard and his rocket

9 TRAVEL GUIDE

Set out in search of whales and seals off Cape Cod. Check out the world's largest collection of dinosaur footprints. Take in a major league baseball game. Go Sox! **104**

PROJECT ROOM

★

MAINE

VERMONT

NEW HAMPSHIRE

ATLANTIC
OCEAN

Natural Bridge
State Park

NEW
YORK

♦ NORTH ADAMS
Berkshire
Taconic Region

The Big Chair

Concord and
Lexington

Walden Pond

LOWELL

GLOUCESTER

♦
Mount
Greylock

♦
○ PITTSFIELD

Connecticut

Connecticut Valley

♦
LEMINSTER ○

♦
LEXINGTON

SALEM
♦
Old North
Church,
Boston

MASSACHUSETTS

WORCESTER ○

Harvard
University

Charles

★ ♦
BOSTON

♦
SPRINGFIELD

Naismith
Memorial
Basketball
Hall of Fame

VE RI
TAS
HARVARD

Boston Common

○ PLYMOUTH

Provincetown
♦

CAPE COD
BAY

RHODE
ISLAND

CONNECTICUT

NEW BEDFORD
♦

HYANNIS
○

Cape Cod

Aquinnah
Cliffs ♦

New Bedford
Whaling National
Historic Park

Martha's
Vineyard

Nantucket
Island

ATLANTIC
OCEAN

0   20
Miles

N
W   E
S

Welcome to Massachusetts!

HOW DID MASSACHUSETTS GET ITS NAME?

Imagine what Massachusetts was like, hundreds of years ago, long before Europeans arrived—and long before the land was a state. The Algonquin people lived in the area we now call Massachusetts. And in the Algonquin language, *mas* meant "great" and *washcuset* meant "mountain or hill." Historians believe the name refers to the Great Blue Hill, part of the Blue Hills in Milton, Massachusetts. The area was once home to the Massachuset group of the Algonquin. This group lived on the coast, between Cape Ann and Plymouth. When the English arrived, they borrowed the name to establish the Massachusetts Bay Colony. Eventually, this colony became Massachusetts, one of the first 13 states!

8

READ ABOUT

Massachusetts
can boast green
fields and fertile
valleys. This is
an aerial view of
Pioneer Valley in
South Deerfield.

C H A P T E R   O N E

LAND

★

MASSACHUSETTS MAY BE A SMALL STATE, BUT IT IS BRIMMING WITH BEAUTY. Its 10,555 square miles (27,337 square kilometers), feature many different landscapes, from rolling hills to fertile valleys to thick forests. The highest point in the state is Mount Greylock at 3,491 feet (1,064 meters) above sea level. And the lowest point is at sea level, along the Atlantic Ocean. The Bay State has nearly 200 miles (322 km) of coastline. If you were to straighten out all of the inlets and bays in Massachusetts, the coast would extend more than 1,500 miles (2,414 km)!

DISCOVERING MASSACHUSETTS

To cross the state east to west, you'll travel about 190 miles (306 km) before reaching the New York border. Head north and you'll come to Vermont and New Hampshire. Turn south and you'll end up in Connecticut and Rhode Island (two states that are smaller than Massachusetts). To the east is the jagged coastline of the Atlantic Ocean. But wait! There's more. Massachusetts has many offshore islands. At 110 square miles (285 sq km), Martha's Vineyard is the largest. There's also crescent-shaped Nantucket, the Elizabeth Islands (a chain of 22 islands), and many smaller islands.

A TIME OF GLACIERS

Several times in its 4.5-billion-year history, Earth has been plunged into an ice age. An ice age is a period of major global cooling that lasts tens of millions of years. The most recent ice age began about 1.6 million years ago. Temperatures were as much as 27 degrees Fahrenheit (15 degrees Celsius) colder than they are now. Much of North America was frozen. Massachusetts was covered in glaciers, and in some places, they were a mile (1.6 km) thick.

About 11,000 years ago, the last ice age came to an end. As temperatures

Massachusetts Geo-Facts

Along with the state's geographical highlights, this chart ranks Massachusetts's land, water, and total area compared to all other states.

Total area; rank	10,555 square miles (27,337 sq km); 44th
Land; rank	7,840 square miles (20,306 sq km); 45th
Water; rank	2,715 square miles (7,032 sq km); 17th
Inland water; rank	423 square miles (1,096 sq km); 36th
Coastal water; rank	977 square miles (2,530 sq km); 8th
Territorial water; rank	1,314 square miles (3,403 sq km); 8th
Geographic center	In north part of Worcester
Latitude	41° 10' N to 42° 53' N
Longitude	69° 57' W to 73° 30' W
Highest point	Mount Greylock at 3,491 feet (1,064 m) above sea level
Lowest point	Sea level along the Atlantic Ocean
Largest city	Boston
Longest river	Connecticut River, 66 miles (106 km)

Source: U.S. Census Bureau

The state of Massachusetts could fit inside Texas more than 25 times.

Massachusetts Topography

Use the color-coded elevation chart to see on the map Massachusetts's high points (dark red to orange) and low points (green to dark green). Elevation is measured as the distance above or below sea level.

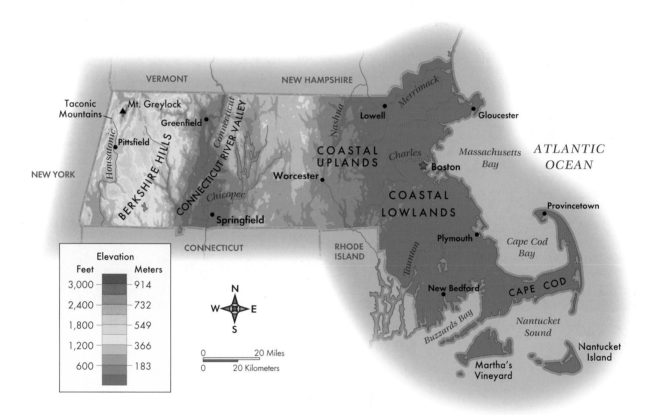

rose, the glaciers began to melt and slide across the landscape, carving out rolling hills and deep valleys in what became the Berkshires in western Massachusetts. Hundreds of small lakes and **kettle ponds** were created in the east, and loose, sandy soil was left behind. The massive runoff of rock and gravel formed the ragged Cape Cod peninsula, Martha's Vineyard, Nantucket, and the state's other offshore islands.

WORD TO KNOW

kettle ponds *ponds that were created when glaciers retreated; most are deep and clean because they are fed by water seeping up through the ground*

Gloucester is one of the major harbors in Massachusetts. Established in 1623, it is the oldest U.S. seaport.

LAND REGIONS

Massachusetts has four major land areas: the Coastal Lowlands, the Coastal Uplands, the Connecticut River Valley, and the Berkshire Hills. Each region has its own distinctive geographic features, plants, and animals.

The Coastal Lowlands

This area covers the eastern third of Massachusetts. To the northeast are the port cities of Gloucester (pronounced GLOSS-ter), Salem, and Newburyport. Forested coves and rocky bays blanket much of the coastline. Trek south along the coast to reach Boston, the capital and largest city in Massachusetts. Continue farther south along the shoreline to reach Plymouth—

where the Pilgrims settled. Head over the Cape Cod Canal by way of Sagamore Bridge to reach Cape Cod in the southeast. You can't miss the bridge or the Cape!

The Cape, as Bay Staters call it, looks like a big fishhook. The natives say it looks like an arm, with Chatham at the elbow. It curves outward into the sea for 65 miles (105 km). The Cape used to be connected to the mainland, but these days a bridge is needed. In the early 20th-century, a 17.4-mile-long (28-km) canal was dug to make it easier for ships to travel up and down the coast. Now ships don't have to go 162 miles (261 km) to get around the Cape or navigate its treacherous waters. On the west side of the Cape, you'll find beaches, salt marshes, and cranberry **bogs**. The sandy soil is perfect for growing blueberries, raspberries, and cranberries. Cranberries are among the state's biggest crops.

Five miles (8 km) off the state's coast, on the island of Martha's Vineyard, you'll find the multicolored Aquinnah Cliffs. The brilliant layers of red, yellow, and green clay, along with white quartz, were formed more than 13,000 years ago by six glaciers.

Cape Cod's cranberry bogs produce this delicious fruit, one of Massachusetts's biggest crops.

WORD TO KNOW

bogs *areas of wet, marshy ground where the soil consists mostly of decomposing plant material*

The Cape Cod Canal separates Cape Cod from the Massachusetts mainland.

SEE IT HERE!

A SWEET PLACE

An oasis of stunning rock formations, valley views, and rare plants can be found at Bartholomew's Cobble. At the 329-acre (133-ha) nature preserve, marble and quartzite rocky knolls, or cobbles, rise above the Housatonic River. The cobbles help produce an alkaline, or "sweet," soil that supports more than 800 different plants. Some are pretty bizarre. The walking fern lives up to its name by rooting the tips of its blades into moss so it can "walk" across a rock face. And the white blossoms of Dutchman's breeches really do look like pants!

WOW

Mount Greylock is the highest point in Massachusetts. Mount Everest, the tallest mountain in the world, is more than eight times taller!

The Berkshire Hills

Western Massachusetts is a breath of fresh mountain air. Forested hills, wetlands, and roving rivers are found in what is known as the Berkshire Taconic region. Here lofty hills climb to more than 2,000 feet (610 m) above sea level. Originally, the Berkshires were tall, rocky peaks, but millions of years of wind, water, and ice wore them down. At 3,491 feet (1,064 m), Mount Greylock is the tallest peak in Massachusetts. The Housatonic River flows south from the Berkshires into Connecticut.

The narrow Taconic Mountains run along the state's western border. Part of the Appalachian Range, the Taconic Plateau is about 6 miles (10 km) wide.

CLIMATE

Writer Mark Twain once said, "If you don't like the weather in New England, just wait a few minutes." It's true. In the Bay State, temperatures can swing by as much as 30 degrees Fahrenheit (17 degrees Celsius) in just a couple of days.

Mount Greylock is 3,491 feet (1,064 m) high. On its summit is the War Veterans Memorial Tower.

Generally, temperatures in the coastal areas are cooler in the summer and warmer in the winter than those in western Massachusetts. Even so, the mercury in Boston can shoot up into the 80s, with high **humidity** to boot, in July and August. Ocean breezes usually keep temperatures hovering in the 70s on the Cape and the islands. Cape Cod gets about 25 inches (64 centimeters) of rain and snow a year, while Boston averages about 42 inches (107 cm) of precipitation annually.

Imagine getting 30 inches (76 cm) of snow in one day! It happened in Gardner on February 6, 2001, setting a new 24-hour state total for snowfall. The Berkshires can get 75 inches (191 cm) or more of the white stuff each season.

Tornadoes

Tornadoes don't strike the Bay State often (the state averages about three twisters per year). But when they do, it can get ugly! On June 9, 1953, a tornado with 260-mile-per-hour (418-kph) winds tore through

Massachusetts is a state that gets hit hard with snow. During the winter months, Bay Staters often have to shovel out through inches, and sometimes feet, of snow.

WORD TO KNOW

humidity *the amount of water vapor in the air; high humidity makes you feel sticky on a hot day*

Weather Report

This chart shows record temperatures (high and low) for the state, as well as average temperatures (July and January) and average annual precipitation.

Record high temperature . . . . 107°F (42°C)
   at New Bedford and Chester on August 2, 1975
Record low temperature . . . . –35°F (–37°C)
   at Chester on January 12, 1981
Average July temperature . . . . 74°F (23°C)
Average January temperature . . . . 29°F (–2°C)
Average yearly precipitation . . . . 42.5 in. (108 cm)

Source: National Climatic Data Center, NESDIS, NOAA, U.S. Department of Commerce

Worcester and surrounding cities. When it was over, 94 people had been killed, 1,300 people were injured, and 10,000 were homeless. Massachusetts ranks 35th in the nation for frequency of tornadoes, but 12th for the amount of damage caused.

Nor'easters

Strong storms called nor'easters are a big threat in Massachusetts. These ice, snow, and rain storms blow in from the North Atlantic packing quite a punch. In February 1978, a nor'easter with 80-mile-per-hour (129-kph) winds dumped 4 feet (1.2 m) of snow on parts of Massachusetts. People watched helplessly as their beachfront homes were washed away. Twenty-nine people lost their lives in that storm.

Hurricanes

Hurricanes pose the greatest threats to the Bay State. Massachusetts has been pummeled by more than a dozen of these violent sea storms since 1900. In 1938, a hurricane slammed into Massachusetts and Rhode Island packing 120-mile-per-hour (193-kph) winds. Storm surges of up to 25 feet (7.6 m) smashed into the coast and islands. Most of New Bedford was submerged under 8 feet (2.4 m) of water! The Connecticut River Valley was soaked by 17 inches (43 cm) of rain, which resulted in widespread flooding. It was one of the most devastating natural disasters in Massachusetts history. In 1954, the state was hit with two hurricanes within two weeks: Hurricane Carol and Hurricane Edna.

Massachusetts National Park Areas

This map shows some of Massachusetts's national parks, monuments, preserves, and other areas protected by the National Park Service.

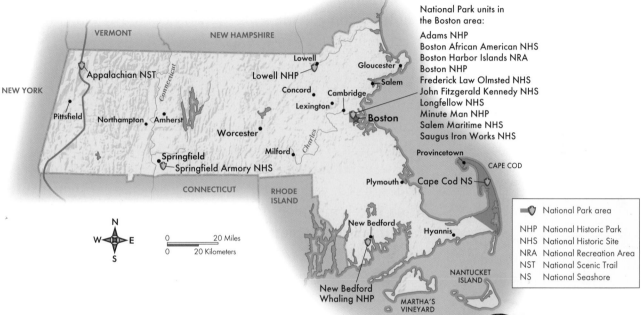

National Park units in the Boston area:

Adams NHP
Boston African American NHS
Boston Harbor Islands NRA
Boston NHP
Frederick Law Olmsted NHS
John Fitzgerald Kennedy NHS
Longfellow NHS
Minute Man NHP
Salem Maritime NHS
Saugus Iron Works NHS

	National Park area
NHP	National Historic Park
NHS	National Historic Site
NRA	National Recreation Area
NST	National Scenic Trail
NS	National Seashore

ANIMAL LIFE

In Massachusetts, you might see the flash of a white-tailed deer bounding through a meadow. In fact, the deer is the most common type of wildlife in Massachusetts. Other large mammals are rare, though there have been sightings of black bears, bobcats, and coyotes in the Berkshires. That area is also home to wild turkeys, warblers, hawks, owls, and the pileated woodpecker.

In the Coastal Lowlands, there are beavers, rabbits, bats, and woodchucks. And the area attracts more than 300 different species of birds! Look up to see black-capped chickadees (the state bird), terns, sparrows, herons, and marsh hawks.

The black-capped chickadee is the state bird of Massachusetts.

ENDANGERED SPECIES

What do the shortnose sturgeon, the lake chub, and the threespine stickleback all have in common? They are endangered species of fish that live in Massachusetts. People throughout the state are working to preserve the environment for these and other endangered animals. Among them are birds such as the peregrine falcon, the upland sandpiper, and the short-eared owl; mammals such as the northern right whale and the humpback whale; and dragonflies such as the zebra clubtail and the coppery emerald. And don't forget the slender walker—that's an endangered snail!

WORD TO KNOW

understory *the layer of plants beneath the shaded area of a forest*

The zebra clubtail dragonfly is one type of endangered animal that lives in the Bay State.

For centuries, fishers have set sail off the coast to catch cod, flounder, haddock, and, at one time, whales. Scallops, lobsters, shrimp, clams, and oysters are also prized. Although fish populations declined in the 20th century, fishing is still a big industry in the Bay State— as is the lure of fresh seafood.

PLANT LIFE

A little more than 60 percent of the land in Massachusetts is covered in forests. In the Berkshires, there's a stunning collection of red oaks, sugar maples, American beech, and sweet birch trees. In the fall, the leaves turn vibrant shades of red, yellow, and gold. It is a spectacular sight! Witch hazel, mountain laurel, and wild azaleas grow in the **understory**. There are also wintergreen, starflowers, Canada mayflowers, and pink lady's slippers.

Pitch pine trees and scrub oaks grow in the Coastal Lowlands, along with marsh grasses, rushes, and sedges. The trailing arbutus, also known as the mayflower (the Massachusetts state flower), was once a familiar sight, but it's now scarce. In the 1700s, people eager to have the fragrant flower in their gardens dug up most of the wild stock.

PROTECTING THE BAY STATE

Did you know that the first environmental law in America was passed in Boston? In 1656, the city made it illegal for butchers to toss waste into Boston Harbor. It didn't help. Other cities kept growing, and they kept dumping their garbage and sewage into the Massachusetts waterways.

With the Industrial Revolution of the 1800s, factories and industries released more pollution into the water. The Bay State's rivers, lakes, swamps, and bogs started to feel the effects. Native plants and animals were harmed. Even today, the piping plover (bird), tiger beetle, eastern puma, bald eagle, and several types of sea turtles and whales remain on the Massachusetts endangered species list—23 species in all.

In the 20th century, people began working to clean up Boston Harbor. They replanted acres of forests once cleared by settlers. Forests now cover more than 3 million acres (1.2 million ha) of Massachusetts—about 60 percent of the state! And the entire Connecticut River Watershed has been designated as a protected **ecosystem**. Things are better, but there is still a long way to go.

A nonprofit conservation group, the Massachusetts Environmental Protection League recently reported that the Bay State's environment is slowly getting worse. Animals, plants, air, soil, and water are being damaged by pollution, development, and other human activities. There is hope, but it means people have to get involved. "All of the problems we chronicle are created by humans, so we are also the answer to these problems," explains Nancy Goodman, the organization's vice president for policy. "By making different choices in our lives and in our public policies, we can ensure a healthy environment for future generations."

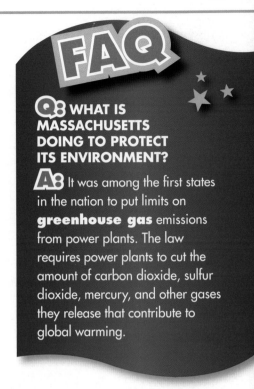

Q8 WHAT IS MASSACHUSETTS DOING TO PROTECT ITS ENVIRONMENT?

A8 It was among the first states in the nation to put limits on **greenhouse gas** emissions from power plants. The law requires power plants to cut the amount of carbon dioxide, sulfur dioxide, mercury, and other gases they release that contribute to global warming.

WORDS TO KNOW

greenhouse gas *a gas that occurs naturally in the atmosphere and contributes to global warming*

ecosystem *a community of plants and animals interacting with their environment*

22

READ ABOUT

Early residents of what is now Massachusetts caught fish by spearing them.

c. 9000 BCE
First humans arrive in Massachusetts

▲ c. 1000 BCE
The Algonquin settle in Massachusetts

▲ 1498 CE
English explorer John Cabot sails along the Massachusetts coast

CHAPTER TWO

FIRST PEOPLE

★

TRY TO IMAGINE WHAT THE WORLD WAS LIKE MORE THAN 11,000 YEARS AGO. That's probably when humans first stepped onto Massachusetts soil. These early settlers are known as Paleo-Indians (*paleo* means "ancient"). Historians debate about where the Paleo-Indians came from—some say the west; others say the south.

1575
Nanapashemet, a Massachuset sachem, is born

c. 1600 ▲
About 12,000 Wampanoag live in southeastern Massachusetts and Rhode Island

1619
Squaw Sachem leads the Massachuset after her husband's death

Bull Brook in Ipswich is one of the largest and oldest Paleo-Indian archaeological sites in North America. Since the 1950s, **archaeologists** have uncovered more than 8,000 artifacts there!

WORD TO KNOW

archaeologists *people who study ancient cultures by examining tools, bones, and other artifacts early humans left behind*

The Algonquin used harpoon points, such as this, to hunt for large game for food and survival.

ANCIENT TIMES

About 11,000 years ago, the last ice age was coming to an end. It was cold in North America. Large mammals, such as mammoths and mastodons, still roamed the earth. Paleo-Indians were nomads. As the seasons changed, the nomads traveled from place to place in search of food. They followed the herds, hunting mammoths, mastodons, caribou, and bison.

In time, other peoples arrived in southern New England. As the climate warmed and glaciers melted, huge herd mammals ceased to exist. To survive, humans had to hunt smaller animals, such as deer, foxes, and raccoons. They also trapped fish and gathered nuts, seeds, and berries.

ALGONQUIN ARRIVAL

About 3,000 years ago, a group of Native Americans traveled from Canada into New England. They were called the Algonquin (also spelled Algonkin). That name means "at the place of spearing fish." The Algonquin *did* excel in spearing fish. But they also used fishing lines and hooks—something the people who'd come to the area before had never done.

Actually, the Algonquin did a lot of things the nomads had never done. They used bows and arrows to hunt deer, bear, moose, and smaller game. They crafted dugout canoes, called *mishoons*, which allowed them to sail offshore to catch turtles and seals. They planted corn, beans, and squash, crops known as "the three sisters." All of these firsts added up to another first—the Algonquin were the first humans to truly settle in Massachusetts. They still traveled to make the most of hunting and fishing seasons, but Massachusetts was their home.

A typical wigwam had a curved surface, which was designed to hold up against the worst weather.

Native American Leaders

Each Algonquin group was led by a chief called a sachem. Typically, it was a man, but women ruled, too. The sachem juggled a lot of duties. This person planned military strategy, supervised the planting and harvesting of crops, and settled disputes among villagers. He or she led celebrations and represented the group when trading with other communities. A council made up of community members often advised the sachem. When a sachem died, a family member usually took over.

Family Ties

To the Algonquin, family was everything—survival depended on it. Frequently, grandparents, parents, and children lived together in a dome-shaped home called a wigwam or *wetu*. The circular frame of the wetu was made from young trees. Men

WOW

Some Algonquin words have become part of the English language, including hickory, moccasin, moose, squash, woodchuck, tomahawk, and powwow.

WHO WERE THE ALGONQUIN OF MASSACHUSETTS?

By the time Europeans arrived in the 1500s, there were seven major tribes in Massachusetts:

Name	Location
Pennacook	Northeast Massachusetts
Nauset and Wampanoag	Southeast Massachusetts, Cape Cod, Martha's Vineyard, Nantucket
Massachuset	Massachusetts's eastern coastline
Nipmuc	Connecticut River Valley
Mohican	The Berkshires
Pocumtuc	Northwest Massachusetts

Native American Peoples
(Before European Contact)

This map shows the general area of Native American people before European settlers arrived.

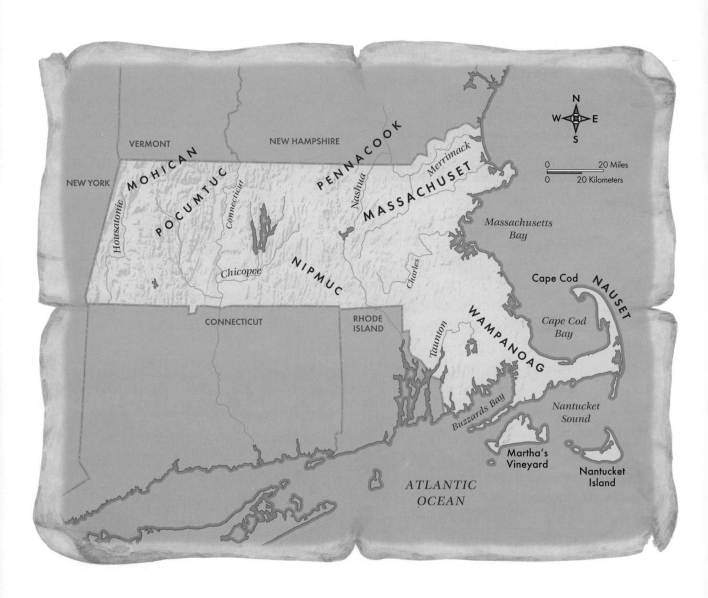

cut the saplings, peeled the bark, and tied the frame together with strips of bark. A large wetu might need 200 saplings! Women wove mats from bark, cattails, or bulrush to cover the walls and roof. A hole in the roof let smoke from the fire escape. And adjustable sheets of bark kept out the rain and snow.

Women looked after the children, tended the crops, cooked, carried water, wove baskets and mats, and made clothing. Men fished, hunted, cleared the land for farming, built wigwams and canoes, and protected their families. Elders sat on tribal councils, taught the children about history, and were respected for their wisdom and knowledge.

Children were considered to be a gift from the Creator. When a child was born, the family celebrated with a big welcoming party. As they grew, Native American children had plenty of time to play. Yet kids were also expected to learn the skills they would need as adults—skills that would ensure the group's survival.

PASSING IT ON

The Algonquin did not have a written language. So everything that mattered—history, traditions, beliefs, and important events—had to be shared through words or artwork. In the evenings, families often gathered

NANAPASHEMET: LAST OF THE MASSACHUSET

One of the last great sachems of the Massachuset people was Nanapashemet (1575–1619). From his main home in Salem, the chief ruled a vast empire. This empire stretched hundreds of miles from the Blue Hills north to the Merrimack River, and from the Atlantic Coast to the Connecticut Valley. With several thousand warriors at his beck and call, Nanapashemet was a respected leader. Even so, the powerful Nanapashemet was helpless against a smallpox infection brought by European trappers. The disease wiped out more than 75 percent of his people in just three years. In 1619, the great chief died at the hands of an enemy tribe. His wife, Squaw Sachem, ruled in his place. But with the loss of so many tribal members, the glory days of the Massachuset were over.

The Wampanoag and other native people used wampum belts. The colors and designs stand for different stories in the group's history.

around the fire. Children listened carefully to the stories their parents and grandparents told about their ancestors. Later, it would be up to them to pass on to their children the tales of great achievements, historic moments, and treasured memories.

The Wampanoag and other coastal groups also kept their heritage alive through wampum. Wampum was strings of purple and white beads made from the shells of hard-shell clams called quahogs. The beads, which were sometimes dyed, were woven onto wampum belts. The different colors and designs stood for various tribal stories, events, and tall tales. Native American historians memorized what each of the designs meant and passed the stories on to the next generation.

By the mid-1800s, few people were left who could speak the complex Wampanoag language. It was in danger of being lost forever. Native American historians looked to documents, including a Bible translated into Wampanoag in the 1650s, for help in recovering the language. Today, many members of the Wampanoag tribe take classes to learn their native tongue.

SPIRITUAL LIFE

Most Native Americans in Massachusetts believed in a Creator. They believed the Creator was present in all of nature's bounty—the rocks, wind, sun, moon, and sea. Families gave thanks each day to the Creator for what they had or were about to receive. If an animal was hunted, special prayers were offered up to the Creator and to the animal's spirit. Also, large thanksgiving ceremonies were held several times throughout the year, usually at harvesttime. Villagers ate, sang, danced, played games, and chanted prayers to show they were grateful for their good fortune.

Algonquin children were taught to have a deep respect for nature. They learned to take only what was needed so there would be plenty for everyone. There were times when tribes clashed over hunting or farming rights, but the land itself was not a possession. After all, they reasoned, how could someone possibly own a meadow or a mountain? In time, Native American peoples learned that not everyone in the world shared their point of view.

Native Americans had many spiritual rituals, including dances such as this one.

30

READ ABOUT

In this detail
from a painting
by William Allen
Wall, Bartholomew
Gosnold, an
English explorer,
makes contact
with the Native
Americans of
Massachusetts.

1602
*Bartholomew
Gosnold explores
Massachusetts Bay*

▲**1620**
*The Mayflower lands
at Provincetown*

1675 ►
*King Philip's
War is fought*

CHAPTER THREE

EXPLORATION AND SETTLEMENT

★

IN 1602, AN ENGLISH EXPLORER NAMED BARTHOLOMEW GOSNOLD SET SAIL ON THE *CONCORD*. He traveled across the Atlantic, reaching a bay on America's eastern seaboard. He called the bay Shoal Hope—but soon changed his mind. After a day of great fishing, during which they caught an abundance of cod, he and fellow sailors altered the name and called it Cape Cod. Gosnold also named Martha's Vineyard and the chain of Elizabeth Islands.

1692
Salem witch trials take place

1775
The American Revolution begins

1788 ►
Massachusetts becomes a state

Today, the town of Gosnold on tiny Cuttyhunk in the Elizabeth Islands has the smallest population of any city in Massachusetts. Just 86 people live there!

WORD TO KNOW

treaty *a written agreement between two or more groups*

MINI-BIO

TISQUANTUM: A FORGIVING SOUL

A Wampanoag named Tisquantum (c. 1580s–1622) was lured, along with 24 other Indians, onto an English ship under the pretext of trading beaver skins. Tisquantum, called Squanto, was captured. British explorers sold Squanto into slavery. He became an interpreter and found his way to Plymouth, where he proved invaluable to the Pilgrim colonists. He taught the English newcomers how to catch fish and also use fish as fertilizer to grow corn, beans, and other crops. Most important, he introduced the colonists to the Wampanoag sachem, Massasoit, and then helped both peoples forge a peace **treaty**. In October 1621, the colonists invited Squanto and other Wampanoag to share their harvest. They feasted on deer, wild birds, fish, corn bread, boiled pumpkin, berries, and nuts. The event is often referred to as America's first Thanksgiving, but it was really just a single festival.

EUROPEANS ARRIVE

Bartholomew Gosnold had discovered what many explorers already knew: America had a rich supply of natural resources. Fish, such as cod and sea bass, were prized in European markets. So was fur. Fur coats and hats were very fashionable in London and Paris. Hunters journeyed to America, trapping beavers, mink, and otters to meet the high demand for fur back home.

In the early 1600s, many of the Algonquin tribes in Massachusetts welcomed the Europeans. But they soon learned to mistrust the new arrivals. Traders and trappers stole their tobacco, canoes, and supplies. They kidnapped tribal members and sold them into slavery. And then there were the diseases. The Indians had no immunity to influenza, smallpox, measles, and other serious infections brought by the Europeans. Epidemics spread rapidly among Indian villages, killing tens of thousands. The Nipmuc, who once numbered about 15,000 in the region, lost 80 percent of their population to disease in a few years. It was the same tragic story for most of the Algonquin.

New Home, Harsh Realities

The *Mayflower* arrived on November 21, 1620, at what is now Provincetown, Massachusetts (on the tip of Cape Cod). Captain Christopher Jones

The passengers of the *Mayflower* arrived in the area of their permanent settlement, Plymouth, on December 11, 1620.

had meant to sail from Plymouth, England, to Virginia, but a storm had blown the ship 200 miles (320 km) off course. Among the 102 passengers were 35 Separatists, a religious group that had broken away from the Church of England. In England, those who didn't agree with the church could lose their lives. America offered the Separatists, and all of the Pilgrims, the chance to start fresh.

John Winthrop coming ashore in Salem, Massachusetts. Winthrop led the Massachusetts Bay Company that settled the Massachusetts area for England.

WORD TO KNOW

colony *a settlement established by a group in a new territory, but with ties to a governing state*

SEE IT HERE!

Plymouth Rock has come to represent the Pilgrims' landing. But in reality, the colonists first set foot on American soil at Provincetown. And none of the colonists' journals mention anything about a rock. Even so, you'll find what's left of the treasured granite symbol under cover on Water Street in Plymouth. Over the years, pieces have been chipped away and sold off as souvenirs. Worse, in an effort to preserve Plymouth Rock, officials kept moving it and breaking it. Historians say less than one-half of the original historic stone remains!

After a number of trips along the coast, the voyagers finally chose a site on Massachusetts's eastern shore to build their permanent **colony**. They named their settlement Plimoth (later spelled Plymouth). Life in the colony was no picnic. The frigid winter weather, lack of adequate food and shelter, and diseases took their toll. "But that which was most sad and lamentable was, that in two or three months' time half of their company died," wrote William Bradford, a Pilgrim who later became governor of the colony.

From a distance, the Wampanoag watched the Pilgrims build their colony. They were used to European trappers coming and going. But staying? *This* was new. In the spring, a Wampanoag sachem named Ousamequin, whom the English came to call Massasoit, decided to invite the colonists to sign a peace treaty. The two sides agreed to protect one another against enemy attack. However, these early gestures of good-will did not last.

Tragic Times

In 1629, England's King Charles granted a group of English investors land in America for a new trad-ing colony. They decided the borders of the new Massachusetts Bay Colony would stretch from 3 miles (4.8 km) north of the Merrimack River to 3 miles (4.8 km) south of the Charles River, and from the Atlantic west to the Pacific. No one knew then that the Pacific Ocean was more than 2,500 miles (4,023 km) away! Boston, established in 1630, became the colony's capi-tal city. Nobody, by the way, bothered to inform the Native Americans of this English land deal.

In the spring of 1630, another religious group from England arrived in Salem to join the Separatists in the Massachusetts Bay Colony. The Puritans thought that followers of the Church of England were too material-istic. They wanted to get back to basics, to live a simple, pure life. Like the Separatists, they hoped to practice their religion freely in America. The problem was that the Puritans tended to treat others as cruelly as they'd been treated. If you disagreed with their views, you could find yourself thrown out of the colony, severely beaten, or hanging by a rope. In 1637, a Puritan named Anne Hutchinson dared to speak out against the strict moral codes set down by Boston's religious leaders. She was tried in court, found guilty, and banished from Massachusetts Bay Colony. Anne's friend Mary Dyer wasn't so lucky. She was hanged.

WITCH HUNT

In January 1692, nine-year-old Betty Parris and her cousin Abigail Williams began acting strangely. Their Puritan community in Salem Village (now Danvers) was certain the girls had been "be-witched." When pressed to name who had cast an evil spell on them, the girls pointed to Tituba, a West Indian woman who was enslaved by Betty's family. Panic spread, and soon people throughout the village were accusing one another of being witches. A court was set up to root out and punish the "witches." In 1693, the governor put a stop to the witch trials, but not before 19 innocent people had been hanged at Gallows Hill.

Anne Hutchinson spoke out against the strict Puritan ways, and she was banished from the colony.

European Exploration of Massachusetts

The colored arrows on this map show the routes taken by European explorers between 1524 and 1620.

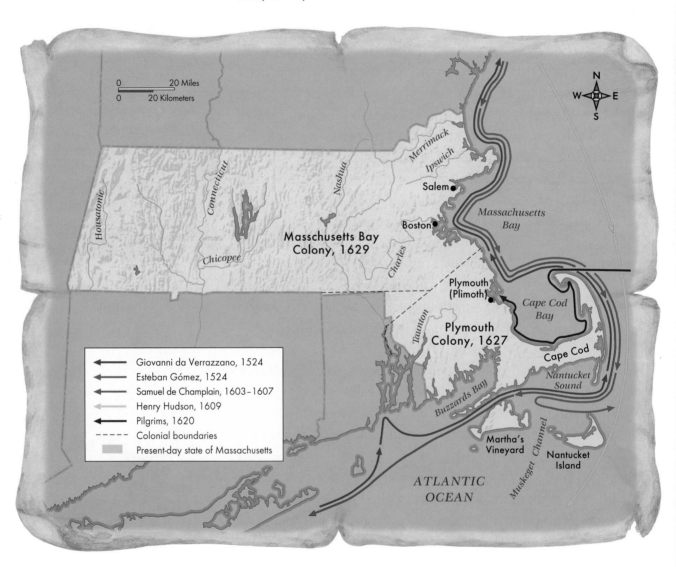

Legend:
- Giovanni da Verrazzano, 1524
- Esteban Gómez, 1524
- Samuel de Champlain, 1603–1607
- Henry Hudson, 1609
- Pilgrims, 1620
- Colonial boundaries
- Present-day state of Massachusetts

Housatonic

Connecticut

Nashua

Chicopee

Merrimack

Ipswich

Salem

Massachusetts Bay Colony, 1629

Boston

Charles

Massachusetts Bay

Plymouth (Plimoth)

Cape Cod Bay

Taunton

Plymouth Colony, 1627

Cape Cod

Nantucket Sound

Buzzards Bay

Martha's Vineyard

Muskeget Channel

Nantucket Island

ATLANTIC OCEAN

When Europeans settled in the Massachusetts Bay Colony in the 1600s, Native Americans suddenly were displaced and were affected by Puritan laws.

THE FIGHT FOR LAND

By the 1640s, nearly 10,000 colonists lived in Massachusetts Bay Colony. More and more, the colonists were settling on land the native people also relied on to survive. The colonial approach to claiming land involved a lot of legal mumbo jumbo and bogus deeds. The Native Americans found themselves trying to follow colonial laws so they could stay on land their ancestors had lived on for generations. It got worse when the Puritans started fining the Indians for breaking their laws, like traveling on the Sabbath. In the 1660s, a Wampanoag sachem named Metacom (sometimes Metacomet) tried to keep the peace treaty his father, Massasoit, had brokered with Plymouth Colony some 40 years earlier. Negotiations didn't go well. When the Puritans refused to stop **encroaching** on tribal lands, the sachem resorted to force to make his point.

> "Against our will these Englishmen take away from us what was our land. They parcel it out to each other, and the marsh along with it against our will."
>
> —FROM A LETTER TO THE GOVERNOR FROM THE WAMPANOAG TRIBE, JUNE 11, 1752

WORD TO KNOW

encroaching *gradually intruding upon or taking away property*

WORD TO KNOW

internment camp *a place where people are confined, usually during wartime*

Metacom, a Wampanoag sachem, was known to the colonists as King Philip.

In 1675, Metacom, whom the colonists called King Philip, led a massive uprising against the colonists. He invaded the town of Swansea, burning part of it. The colonists and British troops retaliated, and King Philip's War was under way. It was a fierce and bloody clash, with many deaths and injuries. By the time the violence ended in 1678, 600 colonists had lost their lives. The Native Americans fared much worse. King Philip was dead, along with several thousand Algonquin. King Philip's War was a blow from which Bay State Indians never recovered. The Wampanoag nation almost died out completely.

The war had shattered all trust between the colonists and the Indians. The colonists were afraid of the Algonquin and wanted them gone. Some of the native peoples fled to join other tribes throughout New England. Others were sold into slavery, forced onto reservations, or executed. Between 500 and 1,000 Nipmuc were marched to an **internment camp** at Deer Island in Boston Harbor. Jailed during the winter months without adequate food, clothing, or shelter, many died. Few ever saw their homeland again.

THE SLAVE TRADE

In the early 17th century, Europeans introduced slavery to America. Historians say African slaves were likely shipped to Massachusetts in the 1620s. But the first recorded instance was found in the journal of John Winthrop, Boston's founder and first governor of the Massachusetts colony. In February 1638, Winthrop wrote that the ship *Desire* arrived from the Caribbean Islands with "some cotton, tobacco, and negroes."

In 1641, Massachusetts became the first colony to legally permit slavery. Merchants in Boston began importing slaves directly from Africa. Often, the slaves were sold in the West Indies for sugar to make rum.

It wasn't uncommon for wealthy families in Boston to own one or two slaves, mainly for household chores. Slavery in Massachusetts was a jumble of contradictions. Slaves were considered to be their masters' property. They could not shop, buy livestock, travel, or even walk the streets alone after 9 P.M. Yet Massachusetts courts defined slaves as people and granted them a few legal rights. Slaves could own property and get wages for overtime work. They could

PHILLIS WHEATLEY: POET WITH HEART

Phillis Wheatley (c. 1753–1784) was just seven years old when she was captured by slave traders in Senegal, Africa, and sold to the Wheatley family in Boston. She spoke no English, but she was a quick learner. The Wheatleys' daughter, Mary, taught her to read and write. A frail young girl, Wheatley had a remarkable gift for poetry. Her Poems on Various Subjects, Religious and Moral was published in London in 1773. This work marked the beginning of African American literature. Wheatley's vivid poems on religion and slavery attracted the attention of Benjamin Franklin, John Hancock, and Voltaire. George Washington so admired her poems he invited her to visit him at his Cambridge headquarters in 1776. No one knows what the general and the slave said about poetry or the American Revolution. In 1773, she was set free. She died six years later at age 31.

 Want to know more? See www.earlyamerica.com/review/winter96/wheatley.html

WORD TO KNOW

discrimination *unfair treatment of a group, often based on gender, race, or religion*

Cape Verdeans were bought and sold into slavery on Cape Cod, specifically for their expertise in fishing and diving. Many of their descendants still live on the Cape.

also file suit in a court of law—which is exactly what slaves Elizabeth "Mumbet" Freeman and Quock Walker did. In 1781, in separate cases, they argued that slavery was illegal under the new Massachusetts Constitution, which was barely a year old. Both won their cases and their freedom!

In 1783, Massachusetts abolished slavery. Fittingly, it was the first state to do so. African Americans in the Bay State, however, had a long uphill battle. Under the law, they still could not vote, go to school, or serve on a jury. They also faced job and housing **discrimination** at every turn. Their fight to live as free American citizens was just beginning.

REVOLUTION!

In 1763, Britain was celebrating a victory. It had defeated France and its Native American allies (the Algonquin among them) in the French and Indian War and won ownership of much of North America. But Britain was in serious financial trouble. King George and Parliament decided to tax the colonists and place British troops in Boston homes. In 1770, Boston colonists, led by Crispus Attucks, a Natick Indian of African descent, pelted British soldiers with snowballs and stones. The British opened fire, killing Attucks and four others. This Boston Massacre became a wake-up call for freedom-seeking Americans.

Between the taxes and the troops, Americans were furious. How dare Britain tax them for importing goods from their motherland? The colonies were not even allowed to send a representative to Parliament. Boston attorney James Otis declared, "Taxation without representation is **tyranny**!" This cry helped spark the Boston Tea Party. Colonists did not want to pay taxes on the tea sitting on ships in Boston Harbor, so they planned a protest. On December 16, 1773, colonists disguised as Mohawks snuck on board three British ships docked in Boston Harbor. The ships held 90,000 pounds (40,823 kg) of imported tea. The colonists dumped every last chest of it into the harbor.

Britain was not amused. It decided to make Massachusetts an example to the rest of the colonies. In 1774, Parliament passed the Intolerable Acts. These restrictions hurt business for the colonists. This legislation closed the port of Boston and sent British troops to occupy the city. Instead of dividing the colonies, however, the Intolerable Acts brought them closer together.

In the fall of 1774, the First Continental Congress met in Philadelphia. Delegates from all the colonies except Georgia showed up. Boston patriot Samuel Adams and his cousin John were among those representing Massachusetts. The congress agreed not to import or export British goods. It insisted Parliament repeal the Intolerable Acts. King George III refused.

On April 18, 1775, British soldiers were ordered to shut down the Massachusetts government. Also, they were supposed to control supplies of guns and gunpowder being stored by the colonies in Concord. Word of their plan leaked out. Patriots Paul Revere, William

WORD TO KNOW

tyranny *a cruel and unfair use of power*

The Boston Tea Party

WORD TO KNOW

militia *an army made up of citizens trained to serve as soldiers in an emergency*

Dawes, and Samuel Prescott rode on horseback throughout the countryside to alert the **militia** that the redcoats [British] were coming! Shots were exchanged between colonial and British soldiers, first at Concord, then at Lexington. The American Revolution had begun!

Picture Yourself...

as a Printer's Apprentice in Colonial Boston

You're a teenage boy, and your parents have arranged for you to be an apprentice to a printer in Boston. It is a contract. The printer will pay your family a little money each week. He will feed and house you and teach you his trade. In return, the printer "owns" you until you reach your 21st birthday. At the print shop, you often put in 14- to 16-hour days, six days a week. At first, you're only allowed to run errands and clean the shop. But after a while, your master teacher begins to show you how to write copy, set type, operate the press, and trim and fold paper. After seven years, you have learned all that your master can teach you. You are a journeyman printer. And you have fulfilled your contract. It's time to go out into the world to earn a living as a printer!

THE ROCKY ROAD TO STATEHOOD

On July 4, 1776, in the midst of the war, the Second Continental Congress adopted the Declaration of Independence. It announced that the colonies were cutting their ties with Britain to form the United States of America. The Declaration did not establish a central government, so each colony, or state, got to rule itself—for the time being. In 1780, the people of the Commonwealth of Massachusetts voted on a state constitution. Written by John Adams, it included a bill of rights. It was so well done that seven years later, it was used as the model for the U.S. Constitution.

After six years of battling the British, the Americans won the war. With the Treaty of Paris, signed in September 1783, Britain acknowledged the colonies were now "free and independent states." At last!

WOW

In Massachusetts, the third Monday in April is a legal holiday called Patriots Day. Schools close in memory of the clashes at Lexington and Concord.

During the American Revolution, colonists gathered to sign the Declaration of Independence in 1776. Thomas Jefferson (standing in orange vest) and Benjamin Franklin (to the right of Jefferson) were leaders in this act.

On February 6, 1788, Massachusetts ratified the U.S. Constitution, becoming the sixth state to join the union. (At this time, what is now Maine was still part of Massachusetts.) A year later, George Washington was elected the first president of the United States. John Adams of Massachusetts was made vice president. In 1797, Adams became the second president of the United States.

In less than 20 years, Massachusetts had gone from a struggling British colony to a full-fledged state in an independent nation. It had played a key role in leading the colonies to freedom. But there was more to come. Much more.

Massachusetts: From Colony to Statehood

(1629–1820)

This map shows the original Massachusetts territory and the area (in yellow) that became the state of Massachusetts in 1788. Until 1820, Maine was part of the state. The state as we know it today is shown in yellow with red lines.

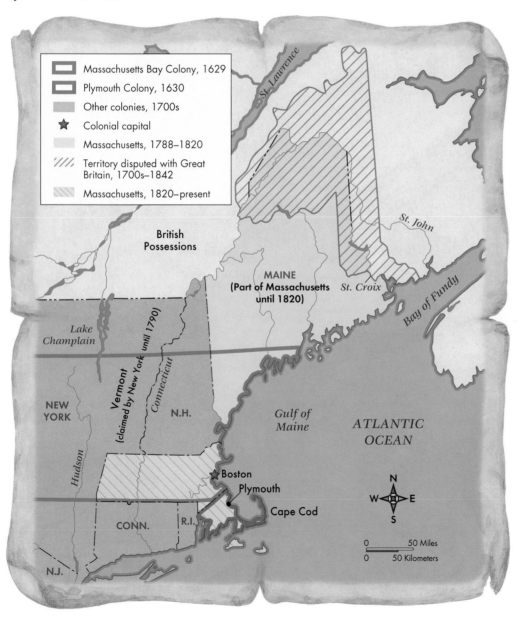

46

Factories were built throughout the growing state. This is the Wason Manufacturing Company in Springfield, which made railroad cars and railway parts.

▲**1793**
*Eli Whitney invents
the cotton gin*

1807
*Congress passes
the Embargo Act*

1813 ▲
*Francis Cabot Lowell opens
the Boston Manufacturing
Company*

C H A P T E R   F O U R

GROWTH AND CHANGE

★

A S THE 19TH CENTURY DAWNED, THE BAY STATE WAS AN EXCITING PLACE TO BE. The industries of farming, fishing, and whaling were thriving. Skilled crafts-people were hand-making furniture, clocks, shoes, and other household goods. Businesses such as shipbuilding and transporting cargo boosted a growing economy.

1836
Massachusetts enacts child labor laws

1852 ▲
Frederick Douglass delivers his famous Fourth of July speech

1861
The 54th Massachusetts Regiment becomes the first African American infantry recruited in the North

WHALING

In colonial times, the oil from sperm whales was highly valued for use in the finest candles, lamps, and perfumes. It sold for $1.77 a gallon (3.8 liters) in 1855. That's almost $40 a gallon in today's currency! At the height of whaling fever, more than 329 whaling ships were based in New Bedford, far more than any other Bay State seaport. Many African and African American sailors were among the crews that served on early whaling ships. The whaling industry quickly made New Bedford one of the richest cities, per capita, in the United States. But the good fortune didn't last long. By the 1870s, overhunting had severely reduced whale populations in the Atlantic. Also, kerosene had begun to replace costly whale oil for lamps. These factors brought an end to the whaling industry by the close of the century.

THE TRADE INDUSTRY

No longer under the thumb of Britain, Massachusetts could trade with any country it wanted to. And it did! Ships sailed out of Boston, Salem, Newburyport, and New Bedford loaded down with cod, whale oil, paper, and tobacco. They headed to ports in Asia, Europe, and the West Indies. They came home with spices, tea, silk, and porcelain from China. They brought molasses and sugar from the West Indies to make rum (much of which was exported to Europe).

However, economic growth in Massachusetts came to a screeching halt in 1807. Britain and France were at

As Boston prospered, it became a busy port city. Ships loaded with goods sailed between the Massachusetts coast and countries around the world.

war. Napoleon, France's leader, refused to let U.S. ships pass his **blockades** to trade with Britain. Not to be outdone, Britain did the same. U.S. president Thomas Jefferson didn't want to get the country tangled up in war, so that year Congress passed the Embargo Act, which stopped all U.S. trade with Europe. Merchants, shippers, and anyone in the Bay State who depended on trade to make a living (and there were a lot of them) were furious. This angry rhyme became popular:

Our ships all in motion once whitened the ocean,
They sailed and returned with a cargo;
Now doomed to decay, they have fallen a prey
To Jefferson—worms—and embargo.

Congress repealed, or dropped, the embargo in 1809. But it took Massachusetts years to bounce back. The War of 1812 didn't help. It sought to stop British interference with U.S. trade. With the British navy blockading many New England ports, it was no surprise that most Bay Staters opposed the war. The War of 1812 ended in a stalemate three years later. A few years later, Maine applied for statehood and split from Massachusetts.

BUSINESS AND INVENTIONS

Brilliant inventors, clever ideas, and America's bulging population of consumers soon had Massachusetts moving in a new direction. Machines that could produce goods faster and cheaper began driving the individual crafter out of the marketplace. In 1793, Westborough native Eli Whitney invented the cotton gin. His machine separated the seeds from cotton fibers a lot faster than could be done by hand. Whitney's cotton gin revolu-

SEE IT HERE!

PRIDE OF THE FLEET

America's USS *Constitution* is one of the oldest commissioned warships in the world. Built in Boston in the 1790s, it took 2,000 trees and $300,000 to build her (silversmith Paul Revere made her copper fastenings). During the War of 1812, the mighty 44-gun ship had the British frigate HMS *Guerriere* waving the white flag of surrender in under a half hour. In the midst of the fighting, an American sailor saw a British cannonball bounce off the *Constitution* and shouted, "Her sides are made of iron!" The nickname "Old Ironsides" stuck. Today, you can tour the ship, fully restored, at Charlestown Navy shipyard in Boston.

IN THE LOWELL MILLS

Young girls and women flocked to Lowell mills to work, happy to leave farm labor. But they soon found the workday began at 4 A.M. and lasted until 7:30 P.M. They also found they had to live in special Lowell boardinghouses under strict supervision, where the food was bread and gravy.

Lowell employees revolted in different ways. They started their own newspaper where they protested, sometimes in poetry, the terrible conditions. Some women were fired for "disobedience," "impudency," and "mutiny." Some organized a **strike** and lost. In 1836, some 1,500 Lowell girls and women formed a Factory Girls Association and called a bigger strike. The strikers marched through Lowell streets singing and protesting harsh working conditions. But their money ran out, they were evicted from their Lowell boardinghouses, and many had to go back to work defeated. But most were still pleased they had shown their independent spirit.

WORD TO KNOW

strike *an organized refusal to work*

Eli Whitney invented the cotton gin in 1793.

tionized the cotton industry by making it cheaper and faster to extract cotton. It led to increased cotton production and more slavery in the southern states.

In 1813, Francis Cabot Lowell opened the Boston Manufacturing Company in Waltham. Built on the Charles River, it was the first factory in America to combine both spinning and weaving in one place. Raw cotton went in, and yards and yards of fabric came out. It was a revolutionary idea. Until then, American mills only spun cotton into thread. Lowell died in 1817, but his "Waltham system" was so successful that his business partners expanded. They built plants in Chicopee, Lawrence, Chelmsford (later renamed Lowell), and Manchester, New Hampshire. In Lowell, a 6-mile-long (9.7-km) canal system was built to run the mills on water power. The plant turned out more than

100 million yards (91 million m) of cloth in 30 years! America's industrial age was off and running.

Children and teenagers worked in the spinning room at the Cornell Mill in Fall River, Massachusetts.

WORKING CONDITIONS

Many factory workers were immigrants from countries such as Ireland, Portugal, Russia, Germany, Poland, Greece, and Italy. Some were young women and children who had been born in America, but had left their families back on the farm for the hope of a better life in the city. Typically, the hours were long, conditions were poor, and the pay was low. A man might put in more than 70 hours a week at a plant—and earn just $8 to $12. Women were paid less than $4 a week. Children, some as young as seven, frequently worked 12 to 14 hours a day, earning a few dollars a week. In 1820, children made up almost half of the workforce in Massachusetts textile mills!

In time, issues such as child labor and women's rights sparked movements in Massachusetts to reform, or improve, society. In 1836, Massachusetts became the

FREEDOM FIGHTERS

In the 1830s, Boston became a center of opposition to slavery. In 1829, David Walker, a free man of color from North Carolina, had published his "Appeal" to his people: "Rise in rebellion" was his message to slaves. This terrified slaveholders, who offered a reward for Walker dead or alive. He died the next year, possibly of poisoning.

In 1831, a young white man, William Lloyd Garrison, published his fiery antislavery paper, *The Liberator*. African Americans helped out as printers. Most of the subscribers came from the black community. Wendell Phillips joined Garrison's antislavery crusade and became one of its leading orators and writers. Runaway slave Frederick Douglass teamed up with Garrison and Phillips. Douglass's stories of his bondage made him one the most significant antislavery writers and speakers.

The Fugitive Slave Law of 1850 permitted slave hunters and U.S. Marshals to seize former slaves and even to demand that citizens assist in the capture of escaped slaves. But Massachusetts said no. It passed a "personal liberty law" that said citizens did not have to cooperate. In Boston, citizens of both races helped slaves escape.

WORD TO KNOW

abolitionist *a person devoted to ending slavery*

MINI-BIO

FREDERICK DOUGLASS: FROM BONDAGE TO FREEDOM

Born into slavery, Frederick Douglass (1818–1895) grew up on a plantation in Maryland. As a boy, he dared to break the rules by learning to read. In 1838, Douglass escaped to freedom, settling in New Bedford. There he began giving lectures and writing about slavery. He helped other slaves escape by opening up his home as a stop on the Underground Railroad, a network of safe houses that helped fugitive slaves reach freedom. When asked to give a Fourth of July speech in 1852, Douglass gave the mostly white audience nothing less than honesty: "What, to the American slave, is your Fourth of July? I answer: a day that reveals to him, more than all other days in the year, the gross injustice and cruelty to which he is the constant victim. To him, your celebration is a sham."

first state to enact child labor laws. It prohibited factories from hiring any child under 15 who hadn't spent at least three months in school the previous year. Horace Mann founded the first board of education. Teacher Dorothea Lynde Dix led the fight to improve conditions in prisons, poorhouses, and psychiatric hospitals. Journalist William Lloyd Garrison published *The Liberator*, an **abolitionist** newspaper. Escaped slave Frederick Douglass gave stirring antislavery speeches and campaigned for

Women ran machines and inspected yarn at the American Woolen Company in Boston.

civil rights for free slaves. Brave leaders such as these were determined to make the Bay State, and the entire country, a better place to live.

MARCHING TO WAR

During the 1800s, the South built its economy on agriculture. Cotton and tobacco were its main crops, and 4 million slaves were used to harvest those crops. The North, by contrast, developed both agriculture and manufacturing. It relied on women, children, and immigrants for its industrial workforce. Slavery was no longer legal in northern states.

Eventually, the clash over slavery (and other rifts, too) led to the South's decision to **secede** and form its own nation. The new president, Abraham Lincoln, was determined to keep the country together. In 1861, he put out the call across the North for military help.

WORDS TO KNOW

civil rights *basic human rights that all citizens in a society are entitled to, such as the right to vote*

secede *to formally withdraw from an alliance*

THE MIGHTY MEN OF THE 54TH

Originally, African Americans weren't allowed to join the Union military. It was believed they weren't brave enough to serve in the armed forces. But as the war raged on and white soldiers were in short supply, the U.S. government changed its tune. In 1863, a young white colonel named Robert Gould Shaw was put in charge of the 54th Massachusetts Regiment, the Union's first African American infantry unit.

The 54th is most remembered for leading the attack on Fort Wagner, South Carolina. Despite taking heavy fire from Confederate troops, the regiment did not surrender. Colonel Shaw and 271 of his 600 soldiers were killed. When the smoke cleared, the 54th Massachusetts Regiment had proven black soldiers did, indeed, have more than enough courage to defend their nation. The film *Glory* (1989), starring Matthew Broderick and Denzel Washington, is based on this historical event.

Massachusetts was the first state to respond and send troops to fight in the Civil War (1861–1865). During the war years, nearly 150,000 soldiers from Massachusetts served in the Union forces. More than 14,000 of them lost their lives.

A TIME OF GROWTH

The Civil War kept Massachusetts factories turning out uniforms, shoes, tents, guns, ammunition, and ships at a record pace. After the North claimed victory, soldiers poured into Massachusetts in search of jobs. At the same time, a new wave of immigrants from Western and Eastern Europe, Asia, and North America (French Canada) began arriving in America. From 1860 to 1890, some 15 million immigrants joined the Massachusetts workforce! They not only found work in the factories,

Salvatore Quattirto worked in the spinning room of Ayer Mill in Lawrence.

but they also built a solid transportation network of roads, canals, and railroads. This era of growth continued, bolstered by yet another clash: World War I.

About 200,000 Massachusetts soldiers fought in World War I (1914–1918). Most served in the 26th Infantry Division, which fired the first American shots in France. During the war years, Massachusetts factories again worked at full throttle to meet the demand for guns, military clothing and supplies, and ships.

By 1920, nearly 4 million people were living in Massachusetts. In just 50 years, the state's population had more than doubled! The 1920 U.S. Census showed that almost 70 percent of Bay Staters were either immigrants or the children of immigrants. Nothing could stop the Bay State's prosperity. Or so it seemed.

Many of the newly arrived immigrants made their way down to Boston's crowded markets each day to work as street vendors. They often hoped to earn enough to start up their own shops or buy homes for their families.

56

Workers took part in the Bread and Roses strike in 1912 to protest unfair employment practices in Lawrence factories. This is the victory parade on Common Street.

1912
The Bread and Roses strike takes place

1926
The Quabbin Reservoir project gets under way

▲ 1929
U.S. stock market crashes

CHAPTER FIVE

MORE MODERN TIMES

★

THE NEW CENTURY WAS A TIME OF PROGRESS AND CHANGE. The 1900s started out rough, but before long the Bay State became a leader in technology and manufacturing. Cities such as Boston, Worcester, and Springfield blossomed, and many people moved to the ever-growing communities surrounding the cities. Massachusetts promised beautiful scenery and all kinds of opportunities.

1942

General Electric scientists test the I-A jet engine

◄**1974**

Federal court orders desegregation of Boston public schools

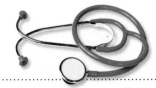

2006▲

Massschusetts becomes the first state in the union to guarantee health care to all citizens

STRIKE!

When workers think their bosses are unfair, they sometimes go on strike. The Bread and Roses strike, one of the biggest in Massachusetts, occurred in 1912. When the state cut the workweek from 56 to 54 hours, textile mill owners in Lawrence sped up the looms (and cut wages). On January 12, more than 23,000 textile workers walked off the job and onto the picket lines. The strikers, most of whom were women, were of 30 different nationalities and spoke 45 languages. The largest groups were German, Italian, French Canadian, and also Poles, Syrians, Turks, Jews, Greeks, Lithuanians, French, and Belgians. They carried signs that read, "We want bread and roses, too!" The slogan meant they wanted fair pay, along with some of the good things in life. Over the next few months, female strikers were beaten, arrested, and even killed by police. Finally, public outcry forced mill owners to give in. The Bread and Roses strike won wage increases and a little more respect for thousands of textile workers across New England.

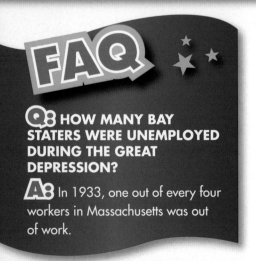

Q8 HOW MANY BAY STATERS WERE UNEMPLOYED DURING THE GREAT DEPRESSION?

A8 In 1933, one out of every four workers in Massachusetts was out of work.

ECONOMIC DECLINE

Until the 20th century, manufacturing and Massachusetts were a perfect match. But slowly, the relationship soured. For one thing, Massachusetts had always focused on just a few products, mainly textiles and shoes. This became a problem in the early 1900s when employers in these industries started pulling up roots in the Bay State to relocate in the South. Why? Money. Southern states were closer to raw materials such as cotton, which meant cheaper shipping costs. Plus, unions in the South weren't as well organized as in the North, so factories could pay employees lower wages. It wasn't long before Bay Staters found there were too many people trying to fill too few jobs.

THE GREAT DEPRESSION

The worst was yet to come. On October 29, 1929, the U.S. stock market crashed. The Boston Stock Exchange lost 25 percent of its value in just two days. The collapse of the U.S. stock market helped plunge the nation into what was known as the Great Depression. Deep in debt after investing in the stock market, banks across the country closed their doors. People lost their life savings when banks closed down. People lost their jobs and homes, and many even lost their confidence because they blamed themselves. The decrease in demand for goods forced Massachusetts's factories and mills to shut down. As shoe plants in Lowell, Lawrence, Lynn, New Bedford, and other towns closed, unemployed factory workers wandered around barefoot.

The Works Progress Administration (WPA) was a New Deal program that employed millions of people throughout the United States. In 1935, these WPA workers helped clean up Lowell after the Merrimack River flooded.

Unemployed people and union members pressured President Frankin D. Roosevelt and Congress to provide relief. So Roosevelt created his New Deal program, which offered jobs, unemployment insurance, and other kinds of social security. One program was the Civilian Conservation Corps (CCC). Members of the CCC created trails on Mount Greylock and built the lodge there. They also developed the Blue Hills Reservation outside Boston. Even so, with 15 million Americans unemployed at the peak of the Depression, it wasn't enough. It took another war to rescue the nation's economy.

WAR, WEAPONS, AND WINGS

When Japan attacked Pearl Harbor, Hawaii, in December 1941, the United States found itself entangled in World War II (1939–1945). While horrific, the

WATER WORKS

The Quabbin Reservoir was designed to meet Boston's increasing demand for drinking water. The project began in 1926, but most of the construction was completed during the 1930s. Creating the lake in central Massachusetts was an answer to prayers for thousands of Bay Staters who needed work during the Great Depression. But it was devastating for those living in the path of construction. Twenty-five hundred residents in the Swift River Valley were sent packing to make way for the reservoir. The towns of Dana, Enfield, Greenwich, and Prescott were destroyed—flooded to create the reservoir. At capacity, Quabbin holds 412 billion gallons (1,560 billion liters) of water!

During World War II, Massachusetts factories were humming, and many of the workers were women.

war did set the Bay State's rusting factories in motion once again. People who'd been devastated by the Great Depression could, at last, earn a living.

During the war years, factories in Worcester, Chicopee, and Springfield turned out rifles and guns. The Springfield Armory alone produced 4.5 million M-1 semiautomatic rifles during the war! Workers used to tuck notes in with the rifles that read, "Dear Son, give 'em hell. Love, Mom." Boston Navy, Fore River, and other shipyards built and repaired warships. More than 32,000 workers, many of them women, kept the Fore River shipyard in Quincy humming. The U.S. government hired private research centers and universities, such as the Massachusetts Institute of Technology (MIT) and Harvard, to develop new defense systems.

On April 18, 1942, scientists at General Electric (GE) in Lynn tested the I-A, the first jet engine ever built in the United States. GE went on to produce some impressive engines for U.S military jet fighters, including the first engines to ever hit speeds of Mach 2 and Mach 3 (two and three times the speed of sound).

Following the war, the state's economy shifted from consumer goods to technology. The state emerged as a leader in computers, aerospace, and medicine. In the 1950s, so many high-tech companies sprang up along Route 128, a road circling Boston, that it became known as America's Technology Highway. Meanwhile, scientists at Harvard and MIT were making great strides in electronics and circuitry.

THE CHALLENGE OF CHANGING

In the 1950s, jobs created by the high-tech industry fueled the Massachusetts economy. Residential areas near Boston grew. Malls, hospitals, schools, restaurants, and other support services sprang up, spawning more jobs. The area was also attracting a new wave of immigrants. People came to the Bay State from Southeast Asia, Central America, Africa, and the Caribbean. The cultures added to the state's diversity, but brought new challenges, as well.

WOW

The world's first computers were built by scientists at Harvard and MIT.

62

MINI-BIO

W. E. B. DU BOIS: WRITER AND ACTIVIST

Born in Great Barrington, W. E. B. Du Bois (1868–1963) graduated at the top of his high school class when he was just 16! On scholarship to Fisk University in Tennessee, Du Bois was shocked by the poverty and racism he saw fellow African Americans enduring in the South. He made it his life's work to study and write about the plight of his fellow African Americans. In 1909, Du Bois was one of the founding members of the National Association for the Advancement of Colored People (NAACP), an organization designed to help improve living and working conditions for people of color. Du Bois's articles and 30 books told truths few people, white or black, knew. He wrote of early, great African civilizations and about the significant role his people played throughout U.S. history. His passionate arguments for racial equality opened the door to the civil rights movement of the 1960s.

 Want to know more? See W. E. B. Du Bois: The Fight for Civil Rights by Ryan P. Randolph (New York: Rosen Publishing Group, 2005).

In the 1960s and 1970s, African Americans and others in the United States were taking a stand for civil rights. It was a turbulent time across the country, filled with protests, tension, and conflict. In 1974, a Massachusetts court ruled the Boston School Committee had not done enough to desegregate schools. Thousands of white students were bused to schools in African American communities, and vice versa. The busing led to conflicts between white and black communities that had been separate for so long.

RECOGNITION FOR NATIVE PEOPLE

In the 1970s, the Wampanoag and Nipmuc nations fought hard to win what is called federal recognition. Unless they were "recognized" as a tribe by the U.S. government, they couldn't get federal money to help with tribal economic development, health care, and education. They also could not reclaim ancient tribal lands. In 1987, the Wampanoag Tribe at Gay Head (Aquinnah) on Martha's Vineyard won federal recognition. Nearly 500 acres (202 ha) of land on the island was returned to them. But four other Wampanoag groups, along with the entire Nipmuc nation, have not been as fortunate and are continuing their quest to be federally recognized. In 2007, the Mashpee community was also recognized as a nation by the U.S. government.

LEADING THE WAY

By 1980, Massachusetts had the lowest unemployment rate in the country. But the boom didn't last. In the late 1980s and early 1990s, the U.S. government made cuts in defense spending. Also, Massachusetts faced competition from other high-tech regions. Growth in the Bay State slowed. Unemployment rose. Today, the state is making a comeback by branching out in new directions. Companies are specializing in areas such as software development, fiber optics, information technology, and **biotechnology**.

From colonial times through the modern age, Massachusetts has made great strides in politics, economics, defense, and civil rights. As the 21st century unfolds, the state continues to forge ahead with new "firsts." In 2006, Massachusetts made headlines when it became the first state in the union to require health care to all its citizens.

WORD TO KNOW

biotechnology *the manipulation of living organisms for developments in the areas of food production, waste disposal, mining, and medicine*

Crowds of people along the banks of the Charles River. As the 21st century began, Massachusetts was a vibrant and ever-changing place.

READ ABOUT

Massachusetts has more than 6 million residents, and many live close to Boston. This is the busy Quincy Market in Boston.

PEOLE

★

HAS ANYBODY INTERESTING COME FROM THE BAY STATE? You bet! The innovative minds behind sewing machines, pink flamingo lawn ornaments, chocolate chip cookies, and the Grinch all hailed from Massachusetts.

Today, more than 6 million people call Massachusetts home—that's a lot of humans for a small state! The Bay State ranks 45th among the states in size, but 13th when it comes to population. Half of all the state's residents live within 50 miles (80 km) of Boston.

Beacon Hill is a neighborhood within Boston that has been home to some of New England's most prominent citizens over the years.

People QuickFacts

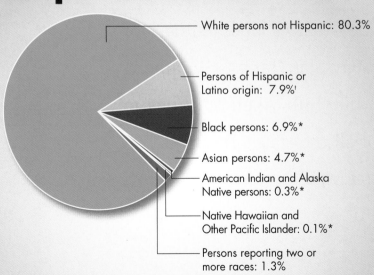

White persons not Hispanic: 80.3%

Persons of Hispanic or Latino origin: 7.9%[1]

Black persons: 6.9%*

Asian persons: 4.7%*

American Indian and Alaska Native persons: 0.3%*

Native Hawaiian and Other Pacific Islander: 0.1%*

Persons reporting two or more races: 1.3%

*Includes persons reporting only one race
[1]Hispanics may be of any race, so they are also included in applicable race categories
Source: U.S. Census Bureau, 2005 estimate

BOSTON BRAHMINS

During America's Industrial Revolution, many of the Protestant descendants of the English colonists in Massachusetts became very wealthy. Among the high and mighty were the Lowells, Cabots, and Lodges. They made their fortunes in textiles, trade, business, banking, and shipbuilding. These ultra-rich, influential families became known as the Boston Brahmins. *Brahmin* is a term that originated in India. It refers to the highest class in a society.

Where Bay Staters Live

The colors on this map indicate population density throughout the state. The darker the color, the more people live there.

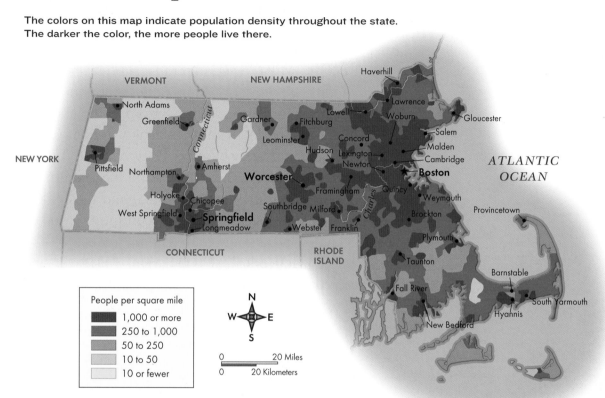

PEOPLE FROM ALL OVER

In the 1840s, a terrible fungus devastated Ireland's main crop, potatoes. To avoid starvation, tens of thousands of Irish people immigrated to America. Many settled in the Boston area with little more than the clothes on their backs. Most weren't educated. Most were Catholic. The Protestant Brahmins looked down on the Irish immigrants. Signs reading "No Irish Need Apply" were a familiar sight in the windows of stores and factories.

In time, the Irish gained a foothold in their new state. They got jobs. They got educated. They became American Citizens and got even with the Brahmins.

WORD TO KNOW

compatriots *people who are born in or have citizenship in the same country*

Some entered politics. With thousands of their Irish **compatriots** behind them, many immigrants were voted into office. They became mayors, senators, and governors. John F. Kennedy, the 35th president of the United States, was the great-grandson of Irish immigrants. Today, 21 percent of Bay State residents claim Irish ancestry—the largest ethnic group in the state.

In the 20th and 21st centuries, new waves of immigrants arrived in Massachusetts. They came from the Caribbean, Puerto Rico, Cuba, Haiti, and the Dominican Republic. People from Vietnam, Korea, and the Middle East also added diversity to the state's community. Today, Boston's largest immigrant group is Haitian. The city also has a fast-growing Brazilian population. Fall River and New Bedford have attracted large numbers of immigrants from Brazil, Portugal, and the Cape Verde Islands (off the western coast of Africa). Lowell has the second-largest

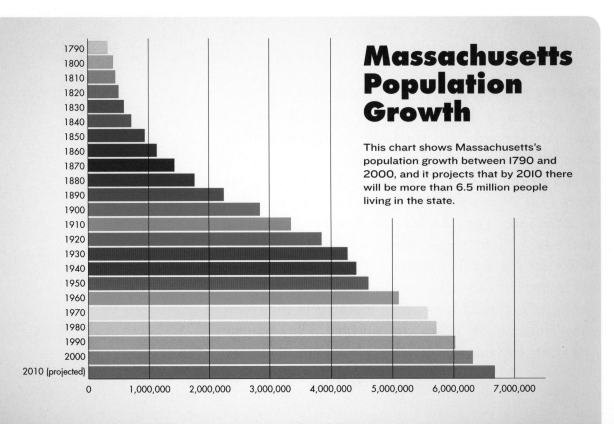

Massachusetts Population Growth

This chart shows Massachusetts's population growth between 1790 and 2000, and it projects that by 2010 there will be more than 6.5 million people living in the state.

This is a scene from a Native American powwow in Worcester.

Cambodian population in the nation. Of the seven Algonquin groups to originally settle in the Bay State, only the Wampanoag and Nipmuc remain today. The Wampanoag has about 3,000 members. Most live in southeastern Massachusetts, Cape Cod, and Martha's Vineyard. The Nipmuc nation numbers about 500 people and is based near Worcester. The Bay State is a blend of various cultures, religions, and races from around the globe.

Big City Life

This list shows the population of Massachusetts's biggest cities.

Boston	.597,763
Worcester	.175,454
Springfield	.151,176
Lowell	.103,229
Cambridge	.101,365
Brockton	.94,191

Source: U.S. Census Bureau, 2006 estimates

MINI-BIO

HORACE MANN: FATHER OF EDUCATION

Growing up in Franklin, Horace Mann (1796–1859) didn't get a formal education, but he loved to read at the town library. He was a quick study and was accepted at Brown University in Rhode Island. In the 1830s, Mann helped set up Massachusetts's first state board of education and public school system. It was used as a model to develop school systems across the nation. As president of Antioch College in Ohio, he made sure women were allowed to take the same courses as men. Just two months before his death, Mann spoke to the graduating class of 1859. Today, his words are spoken at every Antioch graduation: "Be ashamed to die until you have won some victory for humanity."

 Want to know more? See www.pbs.org/onlyateacher/horace.html

THE LEARNING CURVE

Do you know where America's first public elementary school was founded? Massachusetts, of course! The Mather School in Dorchester opened its doors in 1639. The Bay State is also home to the nation's first secondary school (the Boston Latin School) and first university (Harvard College). In the 1850s, Massachusetts became the first state to require all children to go to public school.

Massachusetts has about 120 private and public colleges and universities. Among them are Harvard, MIT, Boston College, Boston University, Brandeis University, Amherst College, Williams College, and the University of Massachusetts. "Go where no one else will go; do what no one else will do," said schoolteacher Mary Lyon. And that's exactly what she did. In the 1830s, Lyon traveled

GREATEST INVENTORS

Some really smart people hail from Massachusetts. Here are some of them, along with their famous inventions.

Benjamin Franklin	lightning rod, bifocal lenses, and the Franklin stove
Samuel Morse	Morse code
Elias Howe	lockstitch sewing machine
Ellen Butterick	tissue paper dress patterns
Alexander Graham Bell	telephone
Lewis Latimer	improved lightbulbs
Edwin Land	Polaroid Land camera

The John Harvard statue overlooks Harvard Yard at Harvard University, one of America's most prestigious institutions.

thousands of miles to raise enough money to establish Mount Holyoke, a private college for women—and she did it 83 years *before* women got the right to vote! Mount Holyoke in South Hadley opened its doors in 1837. It led the way for other women's colleges in Massachusetts, such as Wellesley, Radcliffe, and Smith.

Today, public schools are a top priority in the Bay State. Massachusetts has one of the lowest dropout rates in the country. In 2004, test scores ranked Bay State high school students first in the country in the areas of math and science.

HOW TO TALK LIKE A BAY STATER

Visiting Massachusetts? The Commonwealth has its own slang. Keep this list handy and no one will ever know you're not a true Bay Stater.

barrel: trash can
bubbler: a water fountain
carriage: grocery shopping cart
elastics: rubber bands
frappe: a milkshake or malted
the Hub: Boston
jimmies: chocolate sprinkles
skidder: someone who is always borrowing money from friends
spa: a small convenience store
the T: the Boston subway

Boston cream pie, a classic delectable New England treat

Boston baked beans originated with the Algonquin people.

HOW TO EAT LIKE A BAY STATER

Massachusetts is a great place to be if you're hungry. From one end of the state to the other, there are regional specialties that are the stuff of legend.

Boston baked beans is the dish that first put Boston on the culinary map. After showing the colonists how to grow beans, the Algonquin shared their recipe for cooking them. The Indians slow-cooked their beans in deer hides with maple sugar and bear fat. Bostonians tweaked the recipe, using salt pork and molasses instead.

The official state dessert is another story. Boston cream pie is the creation of French chef Sanzian at the Omni Parker House Hotel in Boston. But did you know that Boston cream pie isn't pie at all? It's a cake. When Sanzian was whipping up his new recipe in 1855, pie tins were easier to come by than cake pans. Have a look at the opposite page to see what else is on the menu in Massachusetts.

MENU

WHAT'S ON THE MENU IN MASSACHUSETTS?

★ ★ ★

Cranberries

Just about any way you like them! Made into juice or put into muffins and bread.

Lobster

A fresh catch from Massachusetts waters, the lobster is a Bay State mainstay. Lobster bakes on the beach—with lobster, hard-shell clams, steamers, mussels, oysters, fish, potatoes, and corn on the cob—are very popular.

Toll House cookies

The accidental invention of a Whitman inn-keeper named Ruth Graves Wakefield, these treats are named for her lodge, the Toll House, located halfway between Boston and New Bedford. Eventually, Wakefield hooked up with the Nestlé Company to get her recipe printed on the back of their candy bars—and in exchange for rights to her recipe, she got a lifetime supply of chocolate chips!

Concord grapes

These were developed by Ephraim Bull in 1829 at his home in Concord. The original vines still grow there! Today, the Concord is one of the most popular grapes used in juices, wines, and jams.

TRY THIS RECIPE
New England Clam Chowder

America's colonists used hard-shell clams (quahogs, remember?) in their traditional English fish and milk stew to create New England clam chowder. The recipe hasn't changed much from the early days. So give this version a try. (Be sure to have an adult nearby to help.)

Ingredients:
- 2 (10-ounce) cans minced clams (drain clams and keep the clam juice)
- 3 cups peeled and cubed potatoes
- 1 onion, chopped
- 1 teaspoon salt
- ¼ teaspoon pepper
- 3 cups milk
- 3 tablespoons flour*

Instructions:

In a large soup pot, combine clam juice, potatoes, onion, salt, and pepper. Bring to a boil. Lower to medium heat and simmer for 15 minutes, or until potatoes are softened. Add milk, flour, and clams. Cover and cook for 5 minutes, or just until heated (don't boil). Enjoy! Serves 4.

* New England clam chowder is typically a thinner soup, but if you prefer a thicker version, you may add more flour, 1 teaspoon at a time, to thicken it.

New England clam chowder

In 2004, the Boston Red Sox won the World Series by defeating the St. Louis Cardinals.

MINI-BIO

TED WILLIAMS: BASEBALL LEGEND

In 1939, a talented young baseball player from San Diego named Ted Williams (1918–2002) was signed by the Boston Red Sox. In his rookie year, the left fielder led the American League with 145 runs batted in (RBIs). The following year, he hit .406 in one season. No professional baseball player had ever hit above .400 before, and no one has done it since. The Kid, or The Thumper as he was also known, played with the Red Sox for 19 seasons. In his career, Williams racked up 2,654 hits, 521 home runs, and a lifetime batting average of .344. Williams retired in 1960 and was inducted into the National Baseball Hall of Fame six years later.

Want to know more? See www.tedwilliams.com/

SPORTS STARS

Boston is a huge sports town. Huge! Especially baseball. Did you know the first World Series was played there in 1903? The Boston Americans took the title, beating the Pittsburgh Pirates five games to three. Today, thousands of die-hard fans pack Fenway Park to see the Red Sox play. Any Bay Stater can tell you how the city went crazy after the team won the 2004 World Series and broke "the curse of the Bambino" (an 86-year World Series dry spell began in 1918 and many believe that the Sox became cursed after trading Babe

Ruth to the New York Yankees in 1920). Some of history's best ballplayers—among them Babe Ruth, Cy Young, and Ted Williams—played for Boston.

When it comes to professional basketball, no National Basketball Association team has racked up more wins than the Boston Celtics—they have 16 NBA titles! Legendary coach Red Auerbach, as well as players Bill Russell, Larry Bird, and 'Pistol' Pete Maravich, were inducted into Springfield's Naismith Memorial Basketball Hall of Fame.

In the National Hockey League, the Boston Bruins are five-time Stanley Cup champions. The New England Patriots, three-time Super Bowl champions, play in Foxborough (south of Boston). The stadium there is also home to the New England Revolution, a Major League Soccer team.

THE LIVELY ARTS

The Bay State has more than 300 museums, including many devoted to children. You can see dinosaurs, reptiles, and a few strange creatures, such as giant tapeworms, at the Harvard Museum of Natural History. Discover the history of manufacturing at Lowell's American Textile History Museum. Journey back to another era at the whaling museums in Salem, Nantucket, and New Bedford. Cape Cod has more than 80 museums!

Speaking of the Cape, Provincetown is home to America's oldest art colony. The Cape Cod School of Art was founded in 1899 and attracted talented artists such as Jackson Pollock and Robert Motherwell. The Cape Playhouse in Dennis is the oldest continuously running professional summer theater in America. It opened on July 4, 1927.

MINI-BIO

THEODOR SEUSS GEISEL: RHYMING WRITER

As a boy in Springfield, Theodor Seuss Geisel (1904–1991) often fell asleep listening to the sound of his mother chanting nursery rhymes. As he got older, he longed to be a cartoonist, but found more success in advertising. In 1937, using the pen name Dr. Seuss, he wrote and illustrated his first book, And to Think That I Saw It on Mulberry Street. He used the same singsong rhyming pattern he remembered from his mom's stories. Twenty-seven publishers rejected the book before one finally said yes. In his lifetime, Dr. Seuss wrote more than 50 books, including classics such as Green Eggs and Ham and The Cat in the Hat. To date, Dr. Seuss's books have sold more than 200 million copies worldwide, and they've been made into cartoons, movies, and even a Broadway show! After his death in 1991, Springfield paid tribute to Dr. Seuss with a bronze sculpture garden featuring some of the author's most beloved characters.

? Want to know more? See www.catinthehat.org/history.htm

ACTORS AND WRITERS

When you go to the movies or watch TV, you may see people with roots in the Bay State. Actors Ben Affleck and Matt Damon were childhood pals in Cambridge. They won an Academy Award for writing the film *Good Will Hunting*. Mark Wahlberg was once known as rap artist Marky Mark, but is now making a name for himself as a film actor. He was born in Dorchester. And talk-show hosts Jay Leno and Conan O'Brien both hail from Massachusetts. Leno was raised in Andover, and O'Brien was born in Brookline.

Massachusetts has produced some of America's finest writers. Emily Dickinson, Ralph Waldo Emerson, Henry David Thoreau, Nathaniel Hawthorne, and Edgar Allan Poe are just a few of its extraordinary literary minds. Louisa May Alcott's *Little Women* was based on her childhood in Concord. Springfield native Theodor Geisel penned more than 50 children's books. You might know him better as Dr. Seuss.

CREATIVE MINDS

Of course, there are plenty of creative types from the Bay State you might not have heard of, though you might recognize their work. In the 1950s, artist Don

Featherstone crafted the first plastic pink flamingo lawn ornament. Since 1957, more than 20 million of the pink plastic birds have been sold. In the 1960s, artist Harvey Ross Ball was hired to design a button that would boost morale at a Worcester insurance company. He doodled a cute yellow smiley face and that did the trick. In eight years, 50 million smiley face buttons were sold in America. Ball never copyrighted his work, so all he made off Smiley was the original $45 he was paid.

Bay Stater Harvey Ross Ball created the smiley face in the 1960s.

Massachusetts is, and always has been, a place where writers, photographers, and artists find magic and inspiration. For more than 20 years, artist Joan Lederman has made her home on Cape Cod. Her studio in Woods Hole is just steps from the sea. She isn't merely influenced by nature; she actually uses it in her artwork. Lederman collects sediments from the ocean floor to create distinctive and dazzling glazes for her pottery. "What appears when I open the kiln is always a surprise," she says.

Massachusetts is an inspiring place for many artists, including this painter in Gloucester.

READ ABOUT

This is the Old
State House in
Boston. On July
18, 1776, from
its balcony, the
Declaration of
Independence was
read aloud to the
people of the city.

CHAPTER SEVEN

GOVERNMENT

★

IN 2004, JUDITH MARCEAU'S THIRD-GRADE CLASS IN GARDNER GOT THE NEWS THEY'D BEEN WAITING FOUR YEARS TO HEAR. Their bill to make blue, green, and cranberry red the official state colors of Massachusetts was signed into law by the governor. Of course, the kids were in the seventh grade by the time it was all made official! As you'll read in this chapter, both kids and adults have a voice in Massachusetts's government.

Capitol Facts

Here are some fascinating facts about Massachusetts's state capitol.

Architect: . . . . Charles Bulfinch
Construction: 1795–1798
Cornerstone laid: . July 4, 1795, by Governor Samuel Adams and Paul Revere
Location: . . . . 24 Beacon Street (built on John Hancock's cow pasture)
Size: . . . . 6.7 acres (2.7 ha)
Number of stories: 3
Dome: . . . . copper, gilded with 23-karat gold leaf
Height of interior dome: . . . . 50 feet (15 m)
Cost of original building: $133,333.33

Massachusetts's constitution is the oldest constitution still in use in the world!

WHERE ALL THE ACTION IS

"Boston State-House is the Hub of the Solar System," wrote Oliver Wendell Holmes in 1858. It was a tiny exaggeration. The State House may not be the center of the universe, but it *is* where most of Massachusetts's political wrangling takes place. The State House on Beacon Hill is hard to miss. It has a 23-karat gold dome with a pinecone emblem on top!

Built in 1795, the new State House on Beacon Hill replaced the Old State House in Boston. The Old State House on Washington Street was constructed in 1713 and remains the oldest public building in the city. Many great historic moments occurred there, from the fiery speeches of patriots denouncing British tyranny to Boston's first public reading of the Declaration of Independence. Today, it is home to the Boston Historical Society and Museum and is surrounded by modern skyscrapers.

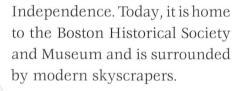

The State House in Boston

THE COMMONWEALTH OF MASSACHUSETTS

You might wonder, What is a commonwealth? It's the same thing as a state. It means "common welfare." John Adams chose the fancy title when he wrote the Massachusetts Constitution in 1780. He thought it best described American democracy in action. Only Massachusetts, Virginia, Kentucky, and Pennsylvania are officially identified as commonwealths.

The state constitution calls for three branches of government, just as the federal system is set up. They are the executive branch, the legislative branch, and the judicial branch.

SEE IT HERE!

SOMETHING'S FISHY

Look up into the gallery of the Massachusetts House of Representatives and you'll see the Sacred Cod suspended from the ceiling. Carved from solid pine, the 4-foot 11-inch (150-cm) cod is a tribute to one of the Bay State's founding industries. Not to be outfished, the Senate hung a wrought-iron chandelier with a fish worked into the design from the ceiling of its chamber. It was dubbed the Holy Mackerel. Take a tour of the State House to see the famous fish.

Capital City

This map shows places of interest in Boston, Massachusetts's capital city.

Massachusetts State Government

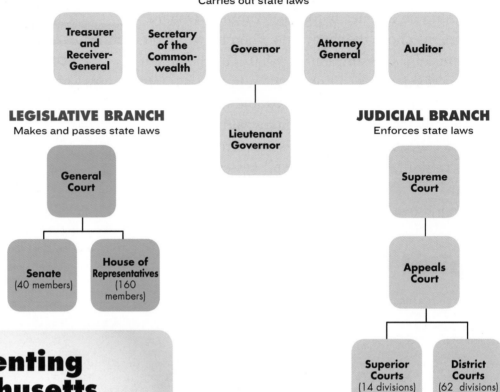

EXECUTIVE BRANCH
Carries out state laws

Treasurer and Receiver-General

Secretary of the Commonwealth

Governor

Attorney General

Auditor

Lieutenant Governor

LEGISLATIVE BRANCH
Makes and passes state laws

General Court

Senate (40 members)

House of Representatives (160 members)

JUDICIAL BRANCH
Enforces state laws

Supreme Court

Appeals Court

Superior Courts (14 divisions)

District Courts (62 divisions)

Representing Massachusetts

This list shows the number of elected officials who represent Massachusetts, both on the state and national levels.

OFFICE	NUMBER	LENGTH OF TERM
State senators	40	2 years
State representatives	160	2 years
U.S. senators	2	6 years
U.S. representatives	10	2 years
Presidential electors	12	—

THE EXECUTIVE BRANCH

The executive branch is headed by the governor. The governor's job is to oversee the state military, prepare the state budget, appoint judges and state department heads, propose laws, and approve or reject new legislation.

THE LEGISLATIVE BRANCH

The legislative branch is the state legislature. It's known as the General Court and is made up of two groups of elected officials: the House of Representatives and the

Senate. The legislature passes laws that are forwarded to the governor for approval. Anyone in Massachusetts can propose a bill, as long as he or she does it through a lawmaker. This is known as the right of free petition. Most bills, however, come from legislators.

In the state house, when a bill is proposed, it goes into a brown box called the hopper. It is assigned a number, gets read out loud on the house floor, and then is sent to a committee for review. After public hearings and further study (which can last a long time), the committee goes before the house or senate to recommend that it be approved or rejected. Members of the house vote electronically by pressing buttons on their desks. Senators vote by voice, saying "yea" or "nay" when their names are called.

When both the house and senate have agreed on a bill, it is sent to the governor. The governor has several options: sign the bill into law, return it to the legislature with suggestions, **veto** it, or refuse to sign it. If the governor refuses to sign a bill, it becomes law anyway after ten days. However, if the legislature adjourns before the ten days have passed, the bill dies. This is known as a pocket veto.

JOHN HANCOCK: AN UNFORGETTABLE NAME

Has anyone ever asked you to "put your John Hancock here"? It means to sign your name, and here's why. At age 27, John Hancock (1737–1793) inherited a ton of money when his uncle passed away. But Hancock didn't squander his fortune. Instead, he joined patriots Samuel Adams, Paul Revere, and James Otis in the fight for American independence. From 1775 to 1777, he was president of the Continental Congress, which was why he got to sign the Declaration of Independence first. Legend has it that he scrawled his name in big letters so King George wouldn't have any trouble reading it. From then on, "John Hancock" became a slang term for a person's signature. In 1780, Bay Staters chose Hancock as their first state governor.

? Want to know more? See www.ushistory.org/declaration/signers/hancock.htm

WORD TO KNOW

veto *to reject a proposed piece of legislation*

BIZARRE BAY STATE LAWS

Most laws make sense, right? But every now and then, a few strange ones slip through the cracks. Here are a few real Massachusetts laws that just might leave you scratching your head:

- English Puritans thought Christmas was a rowdy holiday, so they had it outlawed in Boston from 1659 to 1681; the fine for celebrating was five shillings.
- In the 18th century, if you didn't have cash, you could pay your taxes with beef, iron, or whale oil.
- Dueling with water pistols in Massachusetts is illegal.
- It is against the law to use tomatoes in the production of clam chowder. Note: if you find tomatoes floating in your chowder, you're eating Manhattan clam chowder, not true New England clam chowder.
- At a wake, mourners cannot eat more than three sandwiches.
- You need a license to wear a goatee.

FAQ

Q8 WHEN DID WOMEN ENTER BAY STATE POLITICS?

A8 About two seconds after Congress passed the 19th Amendment to the U.S. Constitution in 1920, giving women the right to vote. In 1921, Massachusetts elected its first female state representatives, Susan Walker Fitzgerald and Sylvia Donaldson. Fifteen years later, Sybil Holmes was the first woman to serve in the senate. The Bay State got its first female governor when Lt. Governor Jane Swift replaced Governor Paul Cellucci, who resigned his post to become U.S. ambassador to Canada in 2001.

THE JUDICIAL BRANCH

The judicial branch refers to the Massachusetts court system, which is set up like a pyramid. At the bottom of the pyramid, seven trial court departments rule on cases involving crime, small claims, contracts, family and juvenile issues, housing, land, and the property of people after they have died. Most appeals from the trial courts move on to be heard by the court of appeals.

The more serious criminal cases skip the appellate court and go right to the top of the pyramid—the supreme judicial court. It's the highest court in the state. The court is a panel of one chief justice and six associate judges. The governor appoints them. The supreme judicial court hears appeals from the lower courts on civil and criminal matters, and agrees with them about 80 percent of the time! The court also establishes rules for the lower courts, and it advises the governor and legislature on legal issues.

Massachusetts Counties

This map shows the 14 counties in Massachusetts. Boston, the state capital, is indicated with a star.

VERMONT NEW HAMPSHIRE

NEW YORK

FRANKLIN

ESSEX

MIDDLESEX

WORCESTER

SUFFOLK

Boston

ATLANTIC OCEAN

BERKSHIRE

HAMPSHIRE

Worcester

NORFOLK

HAMPDEN Springfield

CONNECTICUT

RHODE ISLAND

BRISTOL

PLYMOUTH

BARNSTABLE

DUKES

NANTUCKET

County boundary

0 — 20 Miles
0 — 20 Kilometers

N W E S

THE POLITICAL SPOTLIGHT

Since the 1930s, voters in the Bay State have typically supported Democratic presidential nominees. By the early 21st century, they hadn't voted for a Republican presidential candidate in almost 20 years! Far more Republicans than Democrats, however, have been chosen as governor.

Political Families

Throughout history, some of the country's most influential politicians have come from Massachusetts. In the 18th and 19th centuries, Bay Staters such as Samuel Adams, Benjamin Franklin, James Otis, Paul Revere, and John Hancock took center stage in local and national politics. John Adams and his son, John Quincy Adams,

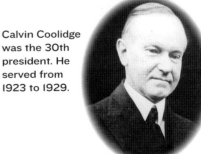

John Quincy Adams was the sixth president of the United States. He served from 1825 to 1829.

Calvin Coolidge was the 30th president. He served from 1923 to 1929.

MINI-BIO

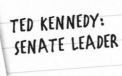

TED KENNEDY: SENATE LEADER

Edward ("Ted") Kennedy (1932–) has represented Massachusetts in the U.S. Senate since 1962. In that year, he was elected to finish the final two years of the Senate term of his brother, John F. Kennedy, who was elected president in 1960. Ted, a leader in the liberal wing of the Democratic Party, is a strong advocate for affordable health care, education reform, civil rights, and defending workers' rights. In 2006, he was chosen as the chair of the Committee on Health, Education, Labor, and Pensions.

? Want to know more? See kennedy.senate.gov/senator/index.cfm

both were elected U.S. president. In the 20th century, the Bay State produced three more presidents: Calvin Coolidge, John F. Kennedy, and George H. W. Bush.

The Kennedys

Few families since the Adamses have had as much impact on American politics as the Kennedys of Massachusetts. John F. Fitzgerald was twice elected mayor of Boston. He was the first son of Irish immigrant parents to hold that office. His grandson, John F. Kennedy, was elected president in 1960. Robert Kennedy, John's brother, was the U.S. attorney general and also a U.S. senator. In 1962, the youngest Kennedy brother, Edward (Ted), was elected to fill the Senate seat of his brother, John, who'd been chosen as president of the United States. Since then, Ted Kennedy has been reelected seven times!

National Politics

Politicians from the Bay State continue to take key roles in national politics. Sometimes, they even battle each other! In 1988, George H. W. Bush (born in Milton) beat three-term Massachusetts governor Michael Dukakis in the U.S. presidential election. In 2004, Massachusetts senator John Kerry won the Democratic nomination. He went toe to toe with George W. Bush (the former president's son) in the race for president, but he lost.

The Presidential Medal of Freedom

MINI-BIO

EDWARD W. BROOKE III: ATTORNEY GENERAL

Edward W. Brooke III (1919–) was a high achiever, even as a kid! He attended Howard University at age 16. Brooke graduated from Boston University Law School and became an attorney, specializing in civil rights and veterans' cases. In 1962, he was elected attorney general of the state of Massachusetts—the first African American attorney general in the state and, for that matter, in the entire United States! Brooke gained a reputation for his tough stand against organized crime and corruption. Four years later, he ran for the U.S. Senate on the Republican ticket and won, becoming the first African American ever elected to the Senate by popular vote. In 2004, the 85-year-old statesman was given the nation's highest civilian award, the Presidential Medal of Freedom.

? Want to know more? See www.abanet.org/publiced/bh_brooke.html

MASSACHUSETTS PRESIDENTS

John Adams (1735–1826) was the second president of the United States. He helped draft the Declaration of Independence and was George Washington's vice president.

John Quincy Adams (1767–1848) was the sixth U.S. president (1825–1829). The son of John Adams, John Quincy was a senator and secretary of state before becoming commander in chief.

(John) Calvin Coolidge (1872–1933) was the nation's 30th president (1923–1929). The former governor of Massachusetts served as vice president and took over the top spot when President Warren G. Harding died in office.

John F. Kennedy (1917–1963) was the 35th U.S. president (1961–1963). At age 43, Kennedy became the youngest person to hold the highest office in the land. He was assassinated in Dallas, Texas, in 1963.

George H. W. Bush (1924–) became the 41st president of the United States (1989–1993). Bush served as vice president under Ronald Reagan for eight years before being elected president. He was born in Milton, but grew up in Connecticut.

88

Governor Deval Patrick (center) with cabinet member Dan O'Connell (left) and Lieutenant Governor Tim Murray (right)

MAKING HISTORY

On November 7, 2006, Deval Patrick was elected governor of Massachusetts. He became the state's first African American governor, as well as the second African American governor in U.S. history. (Doug Wilder of Virginia was the first.) He won the election by a landslide, too. The Harvard-educated lawyer served as assistant U.S. attorney general for civil rights under President Bill Clinton, but he'd never run for office before!

More than 200 years ago, Massachusetts was the birthplace of American politics. Today, its citizens are proud to carry on the grand tradition of serving their state and their country. Who knows? The next president of the United States just might be a Bay Stater. Again!

HOW KIDS GET INVOLVED

As you read earlier, young people in Massachusetts helped designate the state colors. What do those colors mean? Deep blue symbolizes the waters of Massachusetts Bay and the uniforms worn in the American Revolution. Forest green represents the hills of western Massachusetts and the Mohawk Trail. And deep red stands for the state's most abundant crop: cranberries.

Over the years, Massachusetts's students have learned the ins and outs of democracy by working to get new state symbols added to the books. Since the 1970s, they've made the ladybug the state insect, Boston cream pie the state dessert, the corn muffin the state muffin, and the tabby the state cat. More recently, students made basketball the official sport of Massachusetts. The game was invented in 1891 by Springfield teacher James Naismith. With so many young people learning about politics, is it any wonder that Massachusetts has more than 50 state symbols?

Springfield teacher James Naismith invented basketball, the official game of Massachusetts.

State Flag

The Massachusetts flag features the state coat of arms on a white field. The original design dates back to 1915, but the current design—with the shield on both sides of the flag—was approved in 1971.

   The Massachusetts coat of arms consists of a blue shield, a Native American, and a star. The shield of blue represents the Blue Hills of Canton and Milton, Massachusetts. The Native American is a Massachuset, shown carrying an arrow with its tip pointed downward, which indicates he is peaceful. The star represents Massachusetts as one of the 13 original colonies. The motto of the Commonwealth of Massachusetts, *Ense petit placidam sub libertate quietem,* is printed in gold on a blue ribbon. It means, "By the sword we seek peace, but peace only under liberty."

State Seal

The state seal was adopted by Governor John Hancock and the council on December 13, 1780, and made official by the General Court on June 4, 1885. The seal is circular and bears a representation of the Massachusetts coat of arms. Around the coat of arms are the words, *Sigillum Reipublicae Massachusettensis* ("Seal of the Republic of Massachusetts").

READ ABOUT

Harvesting
cranberries
in a Carver,
Massachusetts,
cranberry bog

CHAPTER EIGHT

ECONOMY

★

E VERY DAY, BAY STATERS GET UP AND HEAD TO WORK. Some go to offices or hospitals, and others teach school. Many companies in Massachusetts make things that you use everyday. Did you drink cranberry juice for breakfast? It may have come from Ocean Spray. And did you read a book last night? It may have been published by Houghton Mifflin. And if you wrote a report lately, chances are your printer and its paper came from Staples.

WORKING IN MASSACHUSETTS

Education, health, and social services employ the most workers. Thousands of teachers, administrators, and support staff work in Massachusetts schools. Many educators and researchers have jobs in higher education, working at Harvard, Boston University, and MIT. In just its nuclear science and electronics laboratories, MIT employs more than 17,000 people! Hospitals—such as

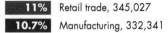

Are you a budding marine biologist? The Woods Hole Oceanographic Institute on Cape Cod is the largest nonprofit marine research facility in the United States.

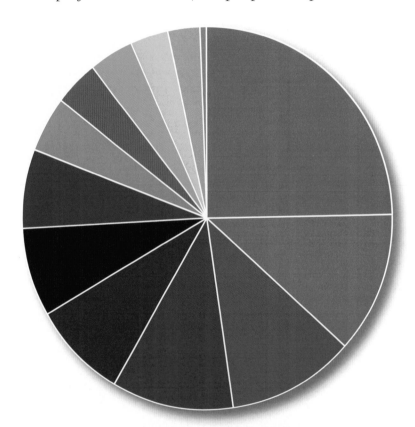

What Do Bay Staters Do?

This color-coded chart shows what industries Bay Staters work in.

24.8% Educational services, health care, and social assistance, 773,218

12.1% Professional, scientific, management, and administrative and waste management services, 377,534

11% Retail trade, 345,027

10.7% Manufacturing, 332,341

8.3% Finance and insurance, and real estate and rental and leasing, 257,729

7.5% Arts, entertainment, recreation, accommodation, and food services, 234,042

6.7% Construction, 210,260

4.5% Other services, except public administration, 139,421

4.0% Public administration, 126,176

3.9% Transportation and warehousing, and utilities, 121,877

3.3% Wholesale trade, 102,015

2.8% Information, 87,265

0.4% Agriculture, forestry, fishing and hunting, and mining, 12,120

Source: U.S. Census Bureau, 2005 estimate

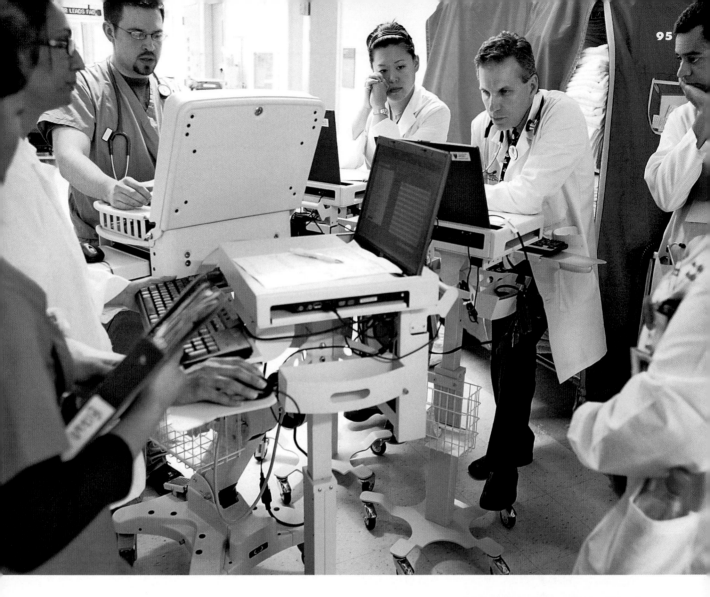

A team of doctors analyzes data at Massachusetts General Hospital. More than 19,500 medical professionals work at Mass General, one of the biggest non-governmental employers in the state.

Massachusetts General (Boston), Brigham and Women's Hospital (Boston), and the University of Massachusetts Memorial Medical Center (Worcester)—are also among the state's major employers.

In the last decade, biotechnology has taken off in the Bay State. In 1991, there were fewer than 100 biotechnology companies in Massachusetts. Today, there are nearly 300, more than anywhere else in the world! Biotechnology companies employ 21,000 Bay Staters directly and another 77,000 people indirectly.

More than half a million people in Massachusetts have jobs in the areas of trade, transportation, and utilities. Did you know Boston was the first city in the country to have a subway? It was built back in 1897. Today, the Massachusetts Bay Transit Authority, or the "T" as it's called, is the nation's fifth-largest transportation system. Every day, 1.2 million passengers hop on buses, streetcars, trolleys, subways, trains, and water ferries to reach 175 cities and towns across the state. About 6,400 people work on the T.

DOING BUSINESS IN THE BAY STATE

There are more than 10,000 manufacturers in Massachusetts. Together, they employ about 400,000 people. The state's main products are no longer shoes and textiles, though these goods are still made. Today's

THE BIG DIG

In 1991, construction began in Boston on the largest public works project ever undertaken in the United States. The Central Artery Tunnel Project, nicknamed The Big Dig, replaced an elevated highway running through Boston with an underground expressway. It also extended Interstate 90 from Boston to Logan International Airport via the new Ted Williams Tunnel. But delays and massive cost overruns plagued the project. In 2004, one of the tunnels started leaking, and in 2006 a cement ceiling tile fell on a car and killed the driver. After repairs were made, the structure reopened to traffic.

The Big Dig Facts:
- Construction dates: 1991– 2005
- Project length: 7.8 total miles (12.6 km) of highway
- Concrete: 3.8 million cubic yards (2.9 million cubic m)
- Estimated cost: $2.5 billion
- Actual cost: $14.6 billion

Trains help Bay State commuters get around every day.

Colorful Sweethearts Conversation Hearts at the NECCO candy factory.

major industries focus on machinery, printing and publishing, and metal fabrication. Scientific instruments, plastic products, and food processing are also key industries.

Two well-known board game manufacturers, Milton Bradley and Parker Brothers, began in Massachusetts, but they are now part of Hasbro in Rhode Island. The New England Confectionary Company (NECCO) is located in Revere. It produces sweet treats like NECCO wafers and Conversation Hearts. Framingham is home to Staples, the huge office supply company. And Houghton Mifflin has a publishing office in Boston.

Nearly 400,000 Bay Staters work in professional and business services, while another 260,000 are employed in finance and insurance. Some of the state's largest

SEE IT HERE!

CHOW DOWN ON CHIPS

Bay Staters swear Cape Cod Potato Chips are the best chips on the planet. More than 250,000 people a year flock to the factory in Hyannis to watch the chip masters turn out 150,000 bags a day. If you take the free tour, you'll get to sample one! Varieties include Sea Salt & Cracked Pepper, Robust Russet, and Reduced Fat Fresh Garden Herb. Try the Beachside Barbecue (yum!).

MINI-BIO

MIKE KITTREDGE: A BRIGHT IDEA

In 1969, Mike Kittredge (1953–) was 16 and didn't have any money to buy a Christmas gift for his mom. So he melted down some wax crayons and made a candle. A neighbor loved his homemade gift and convinced Mike to sell it to her instead. Soon other people in South Hadley were clamoring for Mike's candles. The Yankee Candle Company was off and running. Today, Yankee Candle is the nation's leading scented candle maker, selling 80 million of the scented torches a year! And the flagship store in South Deerfield is the state's second-most popular tourist attraction.

employers include Fidelity Investments, John Hancock Insurance, Raytheon Electronics Systems, and Lucent Technologies (communications) in North Andover.

PERILOUS WATERS

Since the days when Bartholomew Gosnold peered into the waters of Massachusetts Bay and said, "Wow, look at all that cod!" (or something like that), fishing has played a vital role in supporting the Bay State. In the late 1940s, at the height of the commercial fishing industry, Massachusetts fishers were bringing in 650 million pounds (295 million kg) of fish a year! But the boom didn't last—too many fishers were overfishing.

By the 1980s, overfishing caused the state catch to drop to 200 million pounds (91 million kg) a year. The United States passed laws to keep foreign boats out of American waters. It wasn't enough. Officials even restricted the number of days each year a boat could fish, over the objections of some fishers who feared for their livelihoods. It still wasn't enough. Fish populations continued to fall. Today, the commercial fishing industry is alive, but no longer the powerhouse it once was. Fishing makes up just 1 percent of the state's economy.

Cod

Many Bay Staters still rely on fishing to make a living. This fisher works on a trawler off Gloucester.

THINK ABOUT IT!

The Declining Fish Population

Many Bay Staters rely on the fishing industry to make a living. But some people believe that commercial fishing has increased so much over the years that it is destroying the sea environment. Everyone recognizes that the fish population in Massachusetts's waters is on the decline. However, not everyone thinks overfishing is to blame. As Vito Calomo, executive director of the Massachusetts Fisheries Recovery Commission, explains, "The problem is not overfishing. You have to have management rules because there are species that need help, but the major problem is pollution, global warming, [and] destruction of the habitat."

Source: *The Eagle-Tribune* (North Andover)

A COOL IDEA

In the 1920s, an enterprising man named Clarence Birdseye came up with a way to quick-freeze seafood to keep it fresher longer. In 1930, he hit the market with 27 varieties of Birds Eye frozen veggies, fish, and fruit. The frozen food industry was born!

Fresh cranberries bounce! Farmers use bounce boards to help separate good berries from rotten ones, which don't bounce.

FROM CRANBERRIES TO CHRYSANTHEMUMS

If you've ever enjoyed a glass of tangy cranberry juice, there's a good chance it came from Massachusetts. The sandy bogs in southeastern Massachusetts are perfect for growing cranberry vines. Half of the nation's 1,000 cranberry farmers live in Massachusetts. Most operate small family farms. Each year, they work 14,000 acres (5,666 ha) of land to produce about 2 million barrels of the tart, deep red berries. Cranberries grow on long vines in sandy bogs and marshes. Small pockets of air inside the berries allow them to float, so at harvest-time many farmers flood the bogs. Floating booms help gather the berries so they can be sucked up by machines and sent to processing plants.

The Bay State is second only to Wisconsin when it comes to cranberry production. At one time, Massachusetts was the world's top producer. But in the late 1990s, supply outpaced demand, and prices took a nosedive. Cranberry farmers are bouncing back from hard times by creating new ways to use the berries. You'll find 700 different cranberry products on the market today, from mustard to ice cream to hand lotion.

Massachusetts is also a leading producer of blueberries, cousins of the cranberry. The state's

Top Products

Manufacturing machinery, publishing, scientific instruments, food processing
Fishing cod, haddock, halibut, shellfish
Agriculture nursery plants and cut flowers, fruits and vegetables, cranberries
Mining crushed stone, construction sand and gravel

Major Agricultural and Mining Products

This map shows where Massachusetts's major agricultural and mining products come from. See a tree? That means nursery products are raised there.

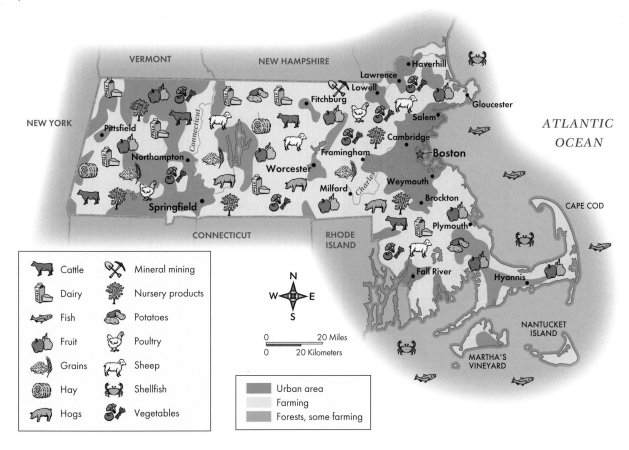

number one agricultural specialty, however, is floriculture: nursery plants and flowers. We're talking potted and hanging plants, annual bedding plants (mums, geraniums, petunias), perennials (flowers that bloom year after year, such as daisies and black-eyed Susans), and cut flowers. Floriculture accounts for a whopping 38 percent of the state's crops, followed by fruits and

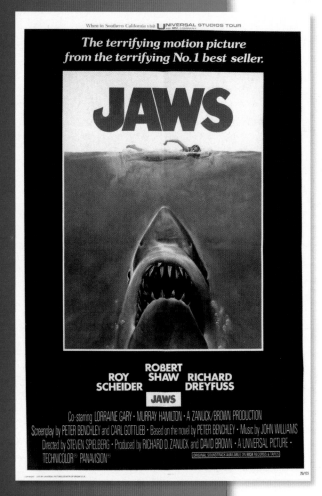

JAWS: BEHIND THE SCENES

One reason Martha's Vineyard was chosen for the setting in *Jaws* was because even 12 miles (19 km) offshore, the water was only 30 feet (9 m) deep. This gave director Steven Spielberg more freedom to use his mechanical shark, nicknamed Bruce. Truth be told, Bruce was broken most of the time.

vegetables (18 percent), cranberries (12 percent), livestock and poultry (12 percent), and milk (11 percent). Only about 14 percent of the state is devoted to farms, and most of them are located in the Connecticut Valley. Agricultural products earn more than $300 million a year for the Bay State.

THE TOURIST INDUSTRY

Each year, about 30 million people travel to Massachusetts. History buffs, sports fans, music and theater lovers, beachcombers, nature lovers, food enthusiasts, shopaholics, and whale watchers (did we forget anyone?) from around the world spend more than $20 billion a year in the Bay State. Restaurants, hotels, small inns, retail shops, artists, and tour guides all depend on precious tourist dollars during the summer months.

Hollywood has also done its part to bring tourists to Massachusetts. For 11 years, *Cheers* was one of the most popular sitcoms on television. It was set in a Boston bar. The Bull and Finch Pub on Beacon Hill inspired the set design for *Cheers*, though the show was taped in Los Angeles (only the exteriors were shot on location). Today, more than half a million people a year head to the place "where everybody knows your name" (the bar changed its name to Cheers to avoid confusion).

Other TV shows set in Massachusetts but usually filmed in Hollywood include *Dawson's Creek, Boston Legal, The Practice, Wings,* and *Crossing Jordan.* Many movies, however, *were* filmed in the Bay State, such as *Legally Blonde, The Perfect Storm,* and *Little Women.*

Perhaps the most famous flick to date was *Jaws*. (Insert scary theme music here!) Much of the 1975 movie about a killer shark attacking people was filmed in and around Martha's Vineyard.

Speaking of Martha's Vineyard, it is one of the Bay State's hottest tourist destinations. During the winter, about 15,000 people call it home, but in the summertime, look out. The population swells to as many as 100,000! The island is only 110 square miles (285 sq km), so you just might bump into some celebrities who like to hang there.

Ready to explore the Bay State for yourself? The next chapter will show you cool places to go and fun things to do in the Commonwealth of Massachusetts. That's right—road trip!

Martha's Vineyard is a big tourist draw. These visitors are enjoying a bike ride in Edgartown.

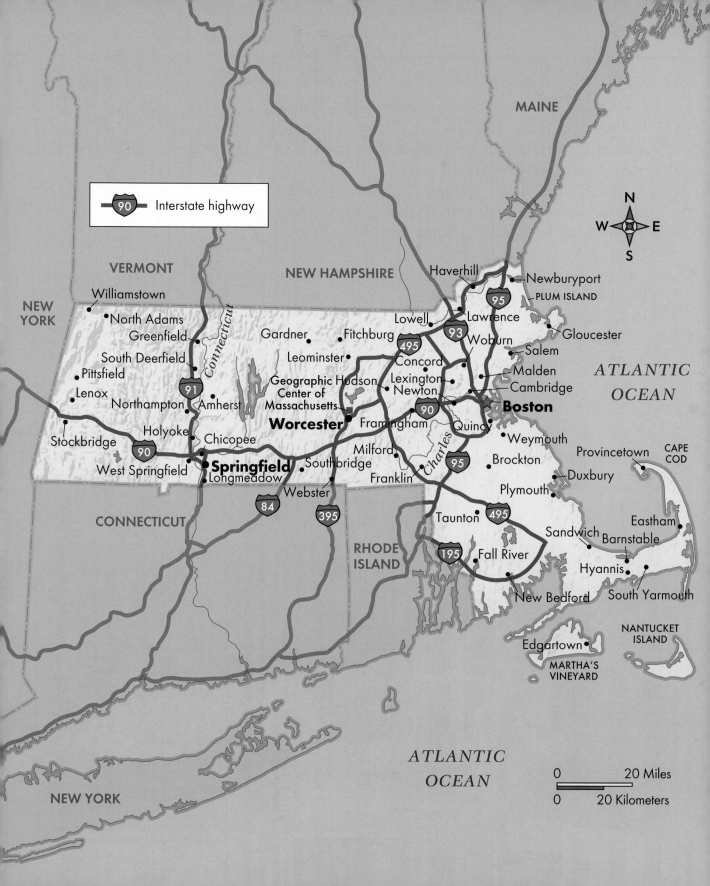

CHAPTER NINE

TRAVEL GUIDE

TRAVEL GUIDE

★

WOULD YOU LIKE TO GO DIGGING FOR CLAMS ON A WINDSWEPT BEACH? How about visiting the site of the first battle of the American Revolution? Maybe you'd rather tour Fenway Park and see the Green Monster for yourself. Or in the summer, you might enjoy a concert under the stars at the Tanglewood Music Center in the Berkshires. You can do all of these things, plus much more, in the Bay State.

← Follow along with this travel map. We'll begin in Boston and travel all around and end in Stockbridge!

BOSTON AND CAMBRIDGE

THINGS TO DO: See a Red Sox game at Fenway Park, or take a walking tour on the Freedom Trail!

Boston

★ **Freedom Trail:** Take a walking tour along some of the most celebrated streets of Boston, which feature a variety of historic sites and landmarks from the American Revolution.

★ **Boston Common:** Enjoy a picnic, pickup football game, or leisurely stroll through one of America's oldest public parks.

★ **Massachusetts State House:** The current home of the Massachusetts Legislature, this house was for-

Boston Public Garden

merly owned by commonwealth governor John Hancock. You can observe a house or senate session to see what important decisions are being made. While you're there, don't forget to look up at the hanging wooden cod in the House of Representatives chamber, which signifies the importance of the fishing industry.

★ **Old State House:** Once it was the center of all political life and debate in colonial Boston. On July 18, 1776, citizens gathered in the streets to hear the Declaration of Independence read from the building's balcony—the first public reading of that document in Massachusetts.

★ **Boston Duck Tours:** Hop on and tour Boston by land and water in a renovated World War II amphibious landing vehicle. You'll cruise by

WHAT IS BOSTON COMMON?

Founded in 1634, the 44-acre (18-ha) green space in Boston is America's oldest public park. The Common was where colonial militia gathered for the Revolutionary War, where abolitionists spoke out against slavery, and where African American leaders such as Martin Luther King Jr. rallied for civil rights. The Common was, and still is, the heart of Boston.

numerous historic sites and be treated to breathtaking views of the city skyline.

★ **Boston Massacre Historic Site:** In front of the Old State House, a circle of cobblestones commemorates the Boston Massacre. It was here that on March 5, 1770, British soldiers fired upon a Patriot uprising and five people were killed.

★ **Paul Revere House:** This is the oldest building in downtown Boston. It was from this home that Revere took off on his famous "midnight ride" to warn the colonist soldiers of the British attack.

★ **Old North Church:** Also known as Christ Church, this historic building was the site of the legendary lantern signal—"one if by land, two if by sea"—on the night of Paul Revere's 1775 ride. Those two lanterns helped the Patriots track the British troops and prepare for the American Revolution.

★ **USS *Constitution*:** The USS *Constitution* is the oldest commissioned warship still afloat in the world. This historic warship is best known for sinking or capturing four British frigates during the War of 1812, thus securing an American victory. A part of American maritime history!

SEE IT HERE!

BLACK HERITAGE TRAIL

Walk Beacon Hill's Black Heritage Trail to explore 14 important sites in African American history. On your journey, you'll see the memorial to the 54th Massachusetts Regiment, the African American meeting-house, and the homes of freed slaves, including Lewis and Harriet Hayden. The Haydens were among the many abolitionists in Massachusetts who opened up their homes as "stops" on the Underground Railroad. By the early 1800s, more than 1,000 former slaves lived in Boston, making it one of the largest free African American communities in the country.

★ **Fenway Park:** One of Boston's, and baseball's, most venerable sites, Fenway Park opened in 1912 and stands as baseball's oldest ballpark that's still in use. Grab a hot dog and watch as hitters try to slug one over the left-field wall, affectionately called the "Green Monster."

★ **New England Aquarium:** Check out the sharks and the sea lions, catch a movie at the IMAX theater, or take a whale-watching cruise.

Humpback whale

★ **John F. Kennedy Library and Museum:** Located on Boston's waterfront, this museum is dedicated to the legacy of President Kennedy. Visitors can experience multimedia exhibits about his life and hear the events of his presidency described in his own voice. From May to October, his sailboat *Victura* is also on display in the harbor.

★ **Museum of Science:** Immerse yourself in the 360-degree experience of the Omnimax Theater, witness a remarkable lightning show, or journey to the far reaches of the universe at the Charles Hayden Planetarium.

Cambridge

★ **Longfellow National Historic Site:** For nine months, this house served as the headquarters of George Washington when he first took command of the Continental Army. It later became the home of world-renowned American poet Henry Wadsworth Longfellow.

★ **Harvard University:** Take a tour of Harvard University, one of the oldest and most prestigious universities in the nation. Make an afternoon visit to the Harvard Museum of Natural History, where you will find exhibits about geology, art, and much more.

NORTH OF BOSTON

THINGS TO DO: Visit the site of the Salem Witch Trials, stop by the House of the Seven Gables, or take a leisurely stroll through the Salisbury Beach State Reservation!

Salem

★ **The House of the Seven Gables:** Built in 1668, this is the oldest surviving 17th-century wooden mansion in New England, and it was the inspiration for author Nathaniel Hawthorne's masterpiece of the same name. Climb the "secret staircase," or stroll through the seaside gardens and along the waterfront.

Harvard University

★ **Peabody Essex Museum:** The museum has one of the most extensive collections of Asian art in the United States. It also presents some of the earliest examples of Native American and Oceanic art in the nation. When you're ready for a breath of fresh air, head outside and walk through one of the lovely gardens.

★ **Salem Witch Museum:** At this museum, you can learn about the history of the Salem witch trials. See what misconceptions led to the events of 1692.

Newburyport

★ **Newburyport Literary Festival:** From fiction to poetry, biographies to nonfiction, this festival features award-winning authors from the area who host readings and discussions of their books and literature. A treat for bookworms of all ages.

★ **Plum Island:** Interested in bird watching? Plum Island is a great place to view your feathered friends. Stroll on the boardwalk, or chill out on the beach. If you're looking for a nice, relaxing afternoon, this is the place to be!

GREATER MERRIMACK VALLEY

THINGS TO DO: Visit Lexington and Concord, where the first shots of the American Revolution were fired, tour the old mills from the early American textile industry, or take a moment to reflect at the famous Walden Pond.

Lexington and Concord

★ **Battle Green:** It was here that the first skirmish between the British and the American Minutemen erupted. You'll see the Minuteman Statue, which memorializes the Lexington Minutemen who lost their lives while fighting the British.

Minuteman statue

★ **Revolutionary Monument:** This is the oldest war memorial and monument in the nation. It is here that the remains of the Patriots slain during the Battle of Lexington were laid to rest.

★ **Hancock-Clarke House:** Where was Paul Revere headed on his midnight ride as he raced to warn Patriots of incoming British forces? The Hancock-Clark House! The residence of John Hancock is filled with furnishings and portraits from the period, including William Diamond's drum and Major Pitcairn's pistols.

★ **Walden Pond:** This placid pond is where Henry David Thoreau mused about nature and was inspired to write his book *Walden*. Enjoy a peaceful and inspiring walk around this literary landmark!

★ **Orchard House:** The historic home of the Alcott family in Concord is where Louisa May Alcott wrote *Little Women*. A visit to Orchard House is like a walk through the book.

Lowell

★ **Boott Mill:** Part of the Lowell National Historic Park, the Boott Mill boardinghouse was home to the "mill girls" who worked in Lowell's factories in the 1800s.

BRISTOL COUNTY

THINGS TO DO: Stroll down the cobblestone streets of New Bedford, visit Seamen's Bethel — the inspiration behind Herman Melville's *Moby-Dick* — and learn about marine life at the New Bedford Whaling Museum!

New Bedford

★ **New Bedford Whaling Museum:** From navigation maps and glass artwork to rare natural history specimens, this is a great place to learn about the importance of whaling in 19th-century New England.

Fall River

★ **Battleship Cove:** Boasting the world's largest collection of historic naval battleships, at Battleship Cove you don't just learn about history— you live it! Experience firsthand what it was like to serve aboard a navy warship in World War II. The adventurous can also explore the submarine USS *Lionfish.*

Plimoth Plantation

PLYMOUTH COUNTY

THINGS TO DO: Climb aboard the *Mayflower II*, experience life as a Pilgrim, or take a walk through one of the oldest homes in the country!

Plymouth

★ **Pilgrim Hall Museum:** As the nation's oldest operating public museum, Pilgrim Hall houses an unmatched collection of Pilgrim possessions. Among priceless treasures you will find here are William Bradford's Bible, Myles Standish's sword, and the only portrait of a Pilgrim (Edward Winslow) painted from life. A fascinating look at what early colonial Pilgrim life was like!

SEE IT HERE!

EXPLORE THE PAST, GLIMPSE THE FUTURE

Want to peek inside a wetu or help make a mishoon? Experience the 17th-century world of the Wampanoag firsthand at the colonial settlement of Plimoth Plantation. At the plantation's English village, actors play the parts of colonists. But you'll find no actors in the re-creation of a Wampanoag home site. Instead, tribal members, dressed in traditional clothing, show visitors how their ancestors lived and worked. They also discuss some of the issues their tribe faces today trying to survive in the modern world.

Duxbury

★ **Alden House Historic Site:** Visit the original homestead of *Mayflower* Pilgrims John and Priscilla Alden. The Aldens were the only family to have lived in this house through four centuries. This historic landmark stands as a testament to early Pilgrim life in America!

CAPE COD

THINGS TO DO: Spend a day at the seashore, savor delicious fresh-caught seafood, hike and bike along scenic trails, or visit one of the Cape's many museums.

Sandwich

★ **Heritage Museums and Gardens:** This quaint museum features exhibits of military miniatures, antique toys, and Native American artifacts. When you've had your fill of the museums, take a walk through the gardens, where you will find pink, purple, and white rhododendrons in bloom!

SEE IT HERE!

CRAZY FOR THE CAPE

With 40 miles (64 km) of protected beaches, the Cape Cod National Seashore is an incredible spot. The 43,000-acre (17,401-ha) park is a collection of swamp forests, salt marshes, meadows, and wild cranberry bogs. There are 365 kettle ponds. In seasonal ponds, called vernal pools, you'll find salamanders, spring peepers (a type of frog), and the rare eastern spadefoot toad.

Cape Cod

Eastham

★ **Cape Cod National Seashore:** Enjoy 40 miles (64 km) of sandy beaches and crashing surf, bicycle and nature trails, marshes, woodlands, and sand dunes. Bring a picnic and spend the day.

Hyannis

★ **John F. Kennedy Hyannis Museum:** This museum features more than 80 photographs spanning the years 1934 to 1963. The collection is arranged in thematic groupings featuring John F. Kennedy, his family, his friends, and the Cape Cod he so dearly loved.

During the busy summer tourist season, 70,000 cars a day cross the three bridges over the Cape Cod Canal.

MARTHA'S VINEYARD

THINGS TO DO: Hop on a ferry and visit the island. Visit the scenic Aquinnah Cliffs, take a spin on the country's oldest operating platform carousel, or stop by the Vineyard museum.

Edgartown

★ **Martha's Vineyard Museum:** This dazzling museum features more than 30,000 items and antiques relating to Martha's Vineyard. There are paintings, prints and sculptures, baskets, coins, costumes, and much more!

★ **Aquinnah Cliffs:** Take in the natural beauty and wonder of the colored clay cliffs of Aquinnah. A great site for aspiring shutterbugs!

Aquinnah Cliffs

SEE IT HERE!

MAGNIFICENT MERRY-GO-ROUND

For more than a century, kids have been hopping on the Flying Horses Carousel in Oak Bluffs on Martha's Vineyard. Built in 1876, it's the nation's oldest platform carousel still spinning. It features intricately painted wooden horses and real stirrups. Catch the special brass ring, and you get a free ride!

★ **Felix Neck Wildlife Sanctuary:** Two miles (3 km) of trails will take you through woodlands, meadows, ponds, salt marshes, and a barrier beach. Listen to the sounds of nature and breathe in the salty air!

NANTUCKET ISLAND

THINGS TO DO: Enjoy sandy beaches and charming lighthouses in this historic port town.

★ **Brant Point Lighthouse:** One of the most photographed lighthouses, this one is also the second-oldest in the United States. You can stroll the grounds and take your own snapshot.

★ **Jetties Beach:** Within walking distance from town, this beach sits on Nantucket Sound so the surf is mild. Enjoy the water, and smell the salty air.

CENTRAL MASSACHUSETTS

THINGS TO DO: Travel to the heart of the state and discover rolling hills and sophisticated cultural attractions.

Amherst

★ **Emily Dickinson Museum:** This museum consists of the Homestead, the poet's home for most of her life, and the Evergreens, her brother's home.

On Elm Street in Gardner, there is a Big Chair. How big? It's 20 feet, 7 inches (6.3 m) tall, and it was once the world's largest.

SEE IT HERE!

DINO PRINTS

Check out the world's largest collection of dinosaur tracks at Amherst College Museum of Natural History. The collection features more than 1,000 fossilized footprints—most of them from the Connecticut Valley!

Naismith Memorial Basketball Hall of Fame

GREATER SPRINGFIELD

THINGS TO DO: Take a roller coaster ride, learn about basketball history, or sail on over to the Titanic Museum.

★ **Naismith Memorial Basketball Hall of Fame:** Check out interactive exhibits, a full multimedia archive, and hundreds of pieces of basketball memorabilia. This museum is a delight for hoops fans of all ages.

★ **Six Flags New England:** Take a ride on one of 10 roller coasters, plunge down Splash Water Falls, then dry off and take in one of the park's many shows.

★ **Titanic Museum:** Discovery, adventure, and education abound at the Titanic Museum. Visitors can see the original blueprints for the ship, a survivor's life jacket, furniture, postcards, menus, and more.

FRANKLIN COUNTY

THINGS TO DO: Take a hike on the historic Mohawk Trail or visit some colorful butterflies.

Greenfield

★ Mohawk Trail: You can enter the trail at a number of spots, but one good starting point is in Greenfield, right in the middle. You can hike east or west along this scenic route, or take a driving tour.

South Deerfield

★ **Magic Wings Butterfly Conservatory and Gardens:** This 18,400-square-foot (1,700-sq-m) conservatory and gardens is home to more than 4,000 free-flying butterflies. Marvel at the beautiful colors of these winged wonders, then relax outside on a park bench and listen to the rush of the waterfalls.

THE BERKSHIRES

THINGS TO DO: Enjoy a summer concert, climb the highest point in the state, and see the works of Norman Rockwell!

Lenox

★ **Tanglewood:** Head over to the Tanglewood Music Center, the summer home of the Boston Symphony Orchestra. Picnic on the lawn while the melodious sounds of the orchestra fill the summer air.

Adams

★ **Mount Greylock:** The highest point in the state, this mountain has absolutely gorgeous views of the surrounding Berkshire Hills!

Williamstown

★ **Sterling and Francine Clark Art Institute:** This art museum houses a breathtaking collection of impressionist art, and can easily inspire all visitors young and old.

Stockbridge

★ **Norman Rockwell Museum:** The museum houses the largest collection of original works by Norman Rockwell, the quintessential American illustrator known for his *Saturday Evening Post* covers.

WRITING PROJECTS

Check out these ideas for creating campaigns and writing you-are-there editorials. Or learn about the state quarter and design your own.

ART PROJECTS

You can illustrate the state song, create a great PowerPoint presentation, or use crafts to tell your family's history.

TIMELINE

What happened when? This timeline highlights important events in the state's history—and shows what was happening throughout the United States at the same time.

FAST FACTS

Use this section to find fascinating facts about state symbols, land area and population statistics, weather, sports teams, and much more.

GLOSSARY

Remember the Words to Know from the chapters in this book? They're all collected here.

SCIENCE, TECHNOLOGY, & MATH PROJECTS 120

Make weather maps, graph population statistics, and research important scientists and inventors from the state.

PRIMARY VS. SECONDARY SOURCES 121

So what are primary and secondary sources and what's the diff? This section explains all that and where you can find them.

BIOGRAPHICAL DICTIONARY 133

This at-a-glance guide highlights some of the state's most important and influential people. Visit this section and read about their contributions to the state, the country, and the world.

RESOURCES

Books, Web sites, DVDs, and more. Take a look at these additional sources for information about the state.

137

WRITING PROJECTS

★ ★ ★

Write a Memoir, Journal, or Editorial for Your School Newspaper!

Picture Yourself . . .

★ As a defense attorney during the Salem witch trials. Keep a journal of your experience.
SEE: Chapter Three, page 35.

★ As a young patriot in the days before the American Revolution. Write a letter to the newspaper, criticizing British policies in Massachusetts.
SEE: Chapter Three, pages 40–42.

★ As a member of the audience during Frederick Douglass's famous Fourth of July speech. Write about your reaction to his ideas.
SEE: Chapter Four, page 52.

★ As Henry David Thoreau, living simply and preserving the environment. If you were on Walden Pond, what would you write about?
SEE: Chapter One, page 15.

★ As a sportswriter, covering the end of the Curse of the Bambino, and the Boston Red Sox and their World Series win in 2004.
SEE: Chapter Six, pages 74–75.

Create an Election Brochure or Web site!

Run for office!

Throughout this book, you've read about some of the issues that concern Massachusetts today. As a candidate for governor of Massachusetts, you need to create a campaign brochure or Web site. Explain how you meet the qualifications to be governor. Talk about the three or four major issues you'll focus on if you are elected. Remember, you'll be responsible for Massachusetts's budget. How would you spend the taxpayers' money?

SEE: Chapter Seven, pages 82–83.

GO TO: Want to know more about what it takes to run the state? Go to Massachusetts's government Web site at www.mass.gov.

Research

Massachusett's State Quarter

From 1999 to 2008, the U.S. Mint introduced new quarters commemorating each of the 50 states in the order that they were admitted into the union. Each state's quarter features a unique design on its reverse, or back.

GO TO: www.quarterdesigns.com/index.html and find out what's featured on the back of the Massachusetts quarter.

Research and write an essay explaining

★ the significance of the image
★ who designed the quarter
★ who chose the final design

What images would you use if you designed the quarter?

ART PROJECTS

★ ★ ★

Create a PowerPoint Presentation or Visitors' Guide

Welcome to Massachusetts!
Massachusetts is a great place to visit and to live! From its natural beauty to its bustling cities and historic sites, there's plenty to see and do. In your PowerPoint presentation or brochure, highlight 10 to 15 of Massachusetts's amazing landmarks. Be sure to include:

★ a map of the state showing where these sites are located

★ photos, illustrations, Web links, natural history facts, geographic stats, climate and weather, plants and wildlife, recent discoveries

SEE: Chapter Nine, pages 105–115.

GO TO: Visit the official Web site of Massachusetts tourism at www.mass-vacation. com. Download and print maps, photos, national landmark images, and vacation ideas.

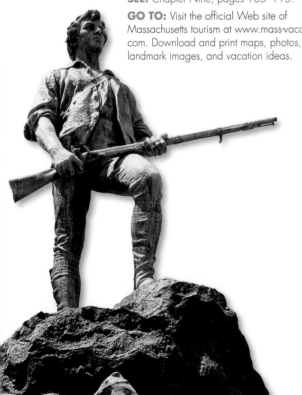

Illustrate the Lyrics to the Massachusetts State Song

("All Hail to Massachusetts")
Use markers, paints, photos, collages, colored pencils, or computer graphics to illustrate the lyrics to "All Hail to Massachusetts," the state song. Turn your illustrations into a picture book, or scan them into PowerPoint and add music!

SEE: The lyrics to "All Hail to Massachusetts" on page 128.

GO TO: Visit the Massachusetts state Web site at www.mass.gov to find out more about the origin of the Massachusetts state song, "All Hail to Massachusetts."

Create a Visual History

Like the early Algonquin, you can use painting, sculpture, quilting, or dance to tell the story of your family history.

SEE: Chapter Two, pages 24–28.

GO TO: Visit the official Web site of the Wampanoag Nation at www.wampanoagtribe. net; the Nipmuc Nation at www.nipmucnation. org; and the Boston Children's Museum at www. bostonchildrensmuseum.org/educators/wampanoag. html to learn more about how the early Algonquin transferred tales and stories into art.

SCIENCE, TECHNOLOGY, & MATH PROJECTS

Graph Population Trends!

Compare population statistics (such as ethnic background, birth, death, and literacy rates) in Massachusetts counties or major cities.

In your graph or chart, look at population density; write sentences describing what the population statistics show; graph one set of population statistics; and write a paragraph explaining what the graphs reveal.

SEE: Chapter Six, pages 67–69.

GO TO: Check out the official Web site for the U.S. Census Bureau at www.census.gov. Find out more about population statistics and how they work, plus the stats for Massachusetts, at quickfacts.census.gov/qfd/states/25000.html.

Create a Weather Map of Massachusetts!

Use your knowledge of Massachusetts's geography to research and identify conditions that result in specific weather events, including hurricanes and nor'easters. What is it about the geography of Massachusetts that makes it vulnerable to severe weather? Create a weather map or poster that shows the weather patterns over the state. To accompany your map, explain the technology used to measure weather phenomena such as blizzards and rainfall and provide data.

SEE: Chapter One, pages 16–18.

GO TO: Visit National Oceanic and Atmospheric Administration's National Weather Service Web site at www.weather.gov for weather maps and forecasts for Massachusetts.

Write a Letter!

Think about some of the brilliant entrepreneurs, scientists, and inventors you've read about in this book—16-year-old Yankee Candle founder Mike Kittredge, rocket scientist Robert Goddard, and many more. Choose one you find especially interesting or inspiring, and write a letter explaining why his or her achievements will continue to touch the lives of generations to come.

SEE: Chapter Five, page 61; Chapter Eight, page 98.

PRIMARY VS. SECONDARY SOURCES

★ ★ ★

What's the Diff?

Your teacher may require at least one or two primary sources and one or two secondary sources for your assignment. So, what's the difference between the two?

★ **Primary sources are original.** You are reading the actual words of someone's diary, journal, letter, autobiography, or interview. Primary sources can also be photographs, maps, prints, cartoons, news/film footage, posters, first-person newspaper articles, drawings, musical scores, and recordings. By the way, when you conduct a survey, interview someone, shoot a video, or take photographs to include in a project—you are creating primary sources!

★ **Secondary sources are what you find in encyclopedias, textbooks, articles, biographies, and almanacs.** These are written by a person or group of people who tell about something that happened to someone else. Secondary sources also recount what another person said or did. This book is an example of a secondary source.

Now that you know what primary sources are—where can you find them?

★ **Your school or local library:** Check the library catalog for collections of original writings, government documents, musical scores, and so on. Some of this material may be stored on microfilm. The Library of Congress (www.loc.gov) is an excellent online resource for primary source materials.

★ **Historical societies:** These organizations keep historical documents, photographs, and other materials. Staff members can help you find what you are looking for. History museums are also great places to see primary sources firsthand.

★ **The Internet:** There are lots of sites that have primary sources you can download and use in a project or assignment.

TIMELINE

★ ★ ★

U.S. Events `1600` **Massachusetts Events**

c. 1600
About 12,000 Wampanoag live in southeastern Massachusetts and Rhode Island.

1602
Bartholomew Gosnold explores Massachusetts Bay; names Cape Cod.

1607
The first permanent English settlement is established in North America at Jamestown.

1619
The first African indentured laborers in English North America are purchased for work in the Jamestown settlement.

1619
Squaw Sachem leads the Massachuset after her husband's death.

1629
Pilgrims found Plymouth Colony, the second permanent English settlement.

1630
Puritans establish Massachusetts Bay Colony, and Boston as its capital city.

1675
King Philip's War is fought.

1682
René-Robert Cavelier, Sieur de La Salle, claims more than 1 million square miles (2.6 million sq km) of territory in the Mississippi River basin for France, naming it Louisiana.

1692
Salem witchcraft trials take place.

`1700`

1773
Colonists rebel with the Boston Tea Party.

1775
The Revolutionary War begins with battles at Concord and Lexington.

1776
Thirteen American colonies declare their independence from Britain, marking the beginning of the Revolutionary War.

U.S. Events

1787
The U.S. Constitution is written.

1803
The Louisiana Purchase almost doubles the size of the United States.

1812–15
The United States and Britain fight the War of 1812.

1830
The Indian Removal Act forces eastern Native American groups to relocate west of the Mississippi River.

1861–65
The American Civil War is fought between the Northern Union and the Southern Confederacy; it ends with the surrender of the Confederate army, led by General Robert E. Lee.

1917–18
The United States is involved in World War I.

Massachusetts Events

1788
Massachusetts becomes the sixth state.

1793
Eli Whitney invents the cotton gin.

1797
John Adams becomes the second president of the United States.

1800

1807
The U.S. Congress passes the Embargo Act.

1813
Francis Cabot Lowell opens the Boston Manufacturing Company.

1820
Maine separates from Massachusetts to become a state.

1825
John Quincy Adams becomes the sixth U.S. president.

1852
Frederick Douglass delivers his famous Fourth of July speech.

1861
The 54th Massachusetts Regiment becomes the U.S. military's first African American infantry unit.

1900

1912
The Bread and Roses strike takes place.

1923
Calvin Coolidge becomes the nation's 30th president.

Adams

U.S. Events

Massachusetts Events

1926
The Quabbin Reservoir project gets under way.

1929
The stock market crashes, plunging the United States into the Great Depression.

1938
The Great New England Hurricane hits.

1941–45
The United States fights in World War II.

1960
John F. Kennedy is elected the 35th U.S. president; Cape Cod National Seashore is established.

1964–73
The United States engages in the Vietnam War.

1967
Edward Brooke III becomes the first African American U.S. senator elected by popular vote.

1974
Federal court orders desegregation of Boston public schools.

1987
Wampanoag Tribe at Gay Head (Aquinnah) receives federal recognition.

1989
George H. W. Bush becomes the 41st U.S. president.

1991
The United States and other nations fight the brief Persian Gulf War against Iraq.

2000

1991
The largest public works project in U.S. history, the Big Dig, breaks ground.

2001
Terrorists hijack four U.S. aircraft and crash them into the World Trade Center in New York City, the Pentagon in Washington, D.C., and a Pennsylvania field, killing thousands.

2004
The Boston Red Sox win the World Series.

2006
Massachusetts elects Deval Patrick as its first African American governor.

GLOSSARY

★ ★ ★

abolitionist a person devoted to ending slavery

archaeologists people who study ancient cultures by examining tools, bones, and other artifacts early humans left behind

biotechnology the manipulation of living organisms for developments in the areas of food production, waste disposal, mining, and medicine

blockades naval ships strategically placed to prevent access to a port

bogs areas of wet, marshy ground where the soil consists mostly of decomposing plant material

civil rights basic human rights that all citizens in a society are entitled to, such as the right to vote

colony a settlement established by a group in a new territory, but with ties to a governing state

compatriots people who are born in or have citizenship in the same country

discrimination unfair treatment of a group, often based on gender, race, or religion

ecosystem a community of plants and animals interacting with their environment

encroaching gradually intruding upon or taking away property

greenhouse gas a gas that occurs in the atmosphere and contributes to global warming

humidity the amount of water vapor in the air; high humidity makes you feel sticky on a hot day

internment camp a place where people are confined, usually during wartime

kettle ponds ponds that were created when glaciers retreated; most are deep and clean because they are fed by water seeping up through the ground

militia an army made up of citizens trained to serve as soldiers in an emergency

secede to formally withdraw from an alliance

strike an organized refusal to work

treaty a written agreement between two or more groups

tyranny a cruel and unfair use of power

understory the layer of plants beneath the shaded area of a forest

veto to reject a proposed piece of legislation

FAST FACTS

★ ★ ★

State Symbols

Statehood date	February 6, 1788; 6th
Origin of state name	Named after local Indian tribe whose name means "great mountain"
State capital	Boston
State nickname	The Bay State
State motto	"By the sword we seek peace, but peace only under liberty"
State bird	Black-capped chickadee
State flower	Mayflower
State fish	Cod
State mineral	Babingtonite
State song	"All Hail to Massachusetts." See lyrics on page 128.
State tree	American elm
State fair	West Springfield (September)

Mayflower,
the state flower

Geography

Total area; rank	10,555 square miles (27,337 sq km), 44th
Land; rank	7,840 square miles (20,306 sq km), 45th
Water; rank	2,715 square miles (7,032 sq km), 17th
Inland water	423 square miles (1,096 sq km); 36th
Coastal water	977 square miles (2,530 sq km); 8th
Territorial water	1,314 square miles (3,403 sq km); 8th
Geographic center	In north part of Worcester
Latitude	41° 10' N to 42° 53' N
Longitude	69° 57' W to 73° 30' W
Highest point	Mount Greylock at 3,491 feet (1,064 m) above sea level
Lowest point	Sea level along the Atlantic Ocean
Largest city	Boston
Number of counties	14
Longest river	Connecticut River, 66 miles (106 km)

Population

Population; rank (2006 estimate)	6,437,193; 13th
Density (2006 estimate)	821 persons per square miles (317 per sq km)
Population distribution (2000 census)	91% urban, 9% rural
Race (2005 estimate)	White persons: 86.7%*
	Black persons: 6.9%*
	Asian persons: 4.7%*
	American Indian and Alaska Native persons: 0.3%*
	Native Hawaiian and Other Pacific Islander: 0.1%*
	Persons reporting two or more races: 1.3%
	Persons of Hispanic or Latino origin: 7.9%†
	White persons not Hispanic: 80.3%

* Includes persons reporting only one race
† Hispanics may be of any race, so they are also included in applicable race categories.

Weather

Record high temperature	107°F (42°C) at New Bedford and Chester on August 2, 1975
Record low temperature	−35°F (−37°C) at Chester on January 12, 1981
Average July temperature	74°F (23°C)
Average January temperature	29°F (−2°C)
Average yearly precipitation	42.5 inches (108 cm)

State seal

Black-capped chicadee, the state bird

State flag

STATE SONG

★ ★ ★

"All Hail to Massachusetts"

Words and music by Arthur J. Marsh

"All Hail to Massachusetts" was adopted as the official song of the Commonwealth on September 3, 1966, and codified by an act of the General Court in 1981.

All hail to Massachusetts, the land of the free and the brave!
For Bunker Hill and Charlestown, and flag we love to wave
For Lexington and Concord, and the shot heard 'round the world;
All hail to Massachusetts, we'll keep her flag unfurled.
She stands upright for freedom's light that shines from sea to sea;
All hail to Massachusetts! Our country 'tis of thee.

All hail to grand old Bay State, the home of the bean and the cod,
Where pilgrims found a landing and gave their thanks to God.
A land of opportunity in the good old U.S.A.
Where men live long and prosper, and people come to stay.
Don't sell her short but learn to court her industry and stride;
All hail to grand old Bay State! The land of pilgrim's pride!

All hail to Massachusetts, renowned in the Hall of Fame!
How proudly wave her banners emblazoned with her name!
In unity and brotherhood, sons and daughters go hand in hand;
All hail to Massachusetts, there is no finer land!
It's M-A-S-S-A-C-H-U-S-E-T-T-S.
All hail to Massachusetts! All hail! All hail! All hail!

NATURAL AREAS AND HISTORIC SITES

★ ★ ★

National Seashore

Cape Cod National Seashore comprises 43,000 acres (17,401 ha) of shoreline. It includes a variety of beaches, salt marshes, freshwater ponds, dunes, and uplands along with many historic buildings, including lighthouses and homes in the Cape Cod architectural style.

National Historic Sites

Massachusetts boasts seven national historic sites. They include *Boston African American National Historic Site*, a 1.6-mile (2.6-km) trail exploring 15 pre–Civil War structures relating to the history of Boston's black community and the African Meeting House, the oldest standing black church in the United States; *John Fitzgerald Kennedy National Historic Site* (Brookline), the birthplace of the 35th president; and *Longfellow National Historic Site* (Cambridge), which celebrates Longfellow's work while at Harvard and the heritage of the great Massachusetts writers of the 19th century, such as Ralph Waldo Emerson and Nathaniel Hawthorne.

National Historical Parks

Five national historical parks are in Massachusetts, including *Adams National Historical Park*, a collection of 11 historic sites over 14 acres (6 ha) of land celebrating the presidents John Adams and John Quincy Adams; *Minute Man National Historical Park* (Lexington and Concord), which preserves the site of the battle that launched the American Revolution; and *New Bedford Whaling National Historical Park*, one of the paramount whaling ports in the 19th century.

State Parks and Forests

Massachusetts has more than 100 state parks, including *Walden Pond, Skinner State Park,* and *Nickerson State Park* on Cape Cod. The largest state forest is *October Mountain State Forest* with more than 16,500 acres (6,677 ha). Since the 1800s, forestland has almost tripled.

SPORTS TEAMS

★ ★ ★

NCAA Teams (Division I)

Boston College *Eagles*
Boston University *Terriers*
Harvard University *Crimson*
College of the Holy Cross *Crusaders*
Northeastern University *Huskies*
University of Massachusetts–Amherst *Minutemen*

PROFESSIONAL SPORTS TEAMS

★ ★ ★

Major League Baseball
Boston Red Sox

National Basketball Association
Boston Celtics

National Football League
New England Patriots

National Hockey League
Boston Bruins

Major League Soccer
New England Revolution

CULTURAL INSTITUTIONS

Libraries

The Harvard University Libraries (Cambridge) are a collection of 90 libraries within the university. Harvard established the first library in the American colonies. Today, it is the largest academic library in the world.

Athenaeum (Boston) contains George Washington's collection of books.

John F. Kennedy Presidential Library and Museum (Boston) contains the papers of the former president.

Boston Public Library is the largest public library in the state.

Museums

Museum of Fine Arts (Boston) has one of the finest collections of Asian art in the world.

Isabella Stewart Gardner Museum (Boston) has many outstanding Renaissance paintings.

George Walter Vincent Smith Art Museum (Springfield), *Worcester Art Museum*, and *Sterling and Francine Clark Art Institute* (Williamstown) are among the nation's best-known smaller museums.

Higgins Armory Museum (Worcester) is devoted to the study and display of arms and armor. Exhibits include such items as helmets of ancient Greece and suits of armor of the Renaissance.

Naismith Memorial Basketball Hall of Fame (Springfield) honors outstanding basketball players and coaches and features exhibits on the history of the game.

Performing Arts

Massachusetts has four major opera companies, two major symphony orchestras, one major dance company, and two professional theater companies.

Universities and Colleges

In 2006, Massachusetts had 31 public and 91 private institutions of higher learning.

ANNUAL EVENTS

January–March

Bay State Games in Williamstown and North Adams (last week in February)

Jimmy Fund "Salute to Winter" Festival Weekend in Holyoke (February)

New England Spring Flower Show in Boston (March)

St. Patrick's Day Parade in Boston (March)

Spring Bulb Show in Northampton (March)

April–June

Boston Marathon (third Monday in April)

Daffodil Festival on Nantucket Island (April)

Hanging of Lanterns in the steeple of the Old North Church in Boston (third Sunday in April)

Reenactment of Paul Revere's Ride in Boston (third Monday in April)

Reenactment of the Battle of Lexington and Concord in Lexington (third Monday in April)

Whale Watch Cruises from Cape Ann to Cape Cod (April–October)

Seaport Festival in Salem (May)

Blessing of Fishing Fleets in Gloucester and Provincetown (late June)

Bunker Hill Day in Charlestown (June 17)

Cambridge River Festival (June)

Cape Cod Chowder Festival in Hyannis (June)

Tanglewood Music Festival in Lenox (mid-June–August)

Williamstown Theatre Festival (June–August)

July–September

Boston Pops Fourth of July Concert on the Boston Esplanade (July)

Esplanade Concerts in Boston (July)

Harborfest in Boston (July)

Up-Country Hot-Air Balloon Fair in Greenfield (July)

Sandcastle and Sculpture Contest in Nantucket (August)

The Big E State Fair in West Springfield (September)

Bourne Scallop Festival in Buzzards Bay (September)

Cranberry Harvest Festival in Harwich (weekend after Labor Day)

October–December

Haunted Happenings in Salem (October)

Head of the Charles Regatta in Boston and Cambridge (October)

Pilgrim Progress Processional and Pilgrim Thanksgiving Day in Plymouth (Thanksgiving Day)

Chowder Contest on Martha's Vineyard (December)

Norman Rockwell's Christmas on Main Street in Stockbridge (December)

John Adams See page 87.

John Quincy Adams See page 87.

Samuel Adams (1722–1803) was a Boston patriot. He was one of the first colonists to suggest a break from British rule, and British officials called him "the most dangerous man in Massachusetts."

Ben Affleck (1972–) is an actor who won an Academy Award for writing the film *Good Will Hunting* (with childhood pal Matt Damon). He was born in California, but grew up in Cambridge and currently has a home there.

Louisa May Alcott (1832–1888) was a writer, most famous for *Little Women*. She lived in Boston and Concord.

Susan B. Anthony (1820–1906) was a women's rights activist who helped secure women's right to vote. She was born and raised in Adams.

Clara Barton (1821–1912) was a teacher and nurse who founded the American Red Cross. She was born in Oxford.

Alexander Graham Bell (1847–1922) was a Boston speech teacher who, in 1876, uttered the first words into a telephone. A year later, the inventor founded the Bell Telephone Company, which became AT&T. He was born in Scotland.

Binh Phu (1970–) is a Vietnamese refugee who came to the United States and graduated from the Culinary Institute of America. In 2005, he opened Hannah's Fusion Bar and Bistro in Hyannis.

Edward W. Brooke III See page 87.

George H. W. Bush See page 87.

Ebenezer Butterick (1826–1903) and **Ellen Butterick (?–1871)** worked to make some of the nation's first tissue paper dress patterns. Ebenezer was born in Sterling.

Steve Carell (1962–) is a comedic actor and writer for both film and TV. He was born in Acton.

Calvin Coolidge See page 87.

John Singleton Copley (1738–1815) was a noted portrait artist who painted pictures of John Hancock, Paul Revere, and other American patriots. He was born in Boston.

Allan Rohan Crite (1910–) is an artist who moved to Boston as a boy. He enjoyed illustrating everyday life in Boston, and today his neighborhood scenes are respected as historical records of the city.

Steve Carell

Louisa May Alcott

Matt Damon (1970–) is an actor who won an Academy Award for cowriting the film *Good Will Hunting* (with childhood pal Ben Affleck). He was born and raised in Cambridge.

Emily Dickinson (1830–1886) was a poet who penned more than 1,700 poems (most weren't discovered until after her death). She was born in Amherst.

Frederick Douglass See page 52.

W. E. B. Du Bois See page 62.

Ralph Waldo Emerson (1803–1882) was a poet and abolitionist. He was born in Boston.

Benjamin Franklin (1706–1790) was a brilliant statesman and scientist who developed such useful items as the lightning rod, bifocal lenses, and the Franklin stove. He was born in Boston, but later lived in Philadelphia.

William Lloyd Garrison (1805–1879) was an abolitionist who founded the antislavery newspaper *The Liberator*. He was born in Newburyport.

Theodor Seuss Geisel See page 76.

Robert Goddard See page 61.

Shirley Ann Jackson

Angelina Weld Grimke (1880–1958) was born in Boston to a family of abolitionists. She was a noted writer and activist during the Harlem Renaissance.

Bob Guillemin (?–) is known as Sidewalk Sam. He's an artist who re-creates some of the world's most famous paintings on Boston street corners.

Matt Damon (left) and Ben Affleck

John Hancock See page 83.

Oliver Wendell Holmes Sr. (1809–1894) was a writer and physician. He was one of the Boston Brahmins.

Winslow Homer (1836–1910) was a landscape artist and printmaker. He is considered one of the most important painters of the 19th century, and some of his best-known works are of the sea. He was born in Boston.

Elias Howe (1819–1867) invented a lockstitch sewing machine that helped revolutionize the clothing and shoe industry. He was born in Spencer.

Anne Hutchinson (1591–1643) was a religious activist who spoke out against strict Puritan laws in Boston.

Shirley Ann Jackson (1946–) was born in Washington, D.C., but she made history in Massachusetts. She was the first African American woman to earn a doctorate at MIT. In 1995, Jackson was appointed as chair of the U.S. Nuclear Regulatory Commission. And in 1999, she was named president of the Rensselaer Polytechnic Institute in Troy, New York.

Edward Kennedy See page 86.

John F. Kennedy See page 87.

Mike Kittredge See page 98.

Edwin Land (1909–1991) was 19 when he patented a plastic sunlight-filtering sheet of crystals and called it Polaroid. Years later, he took a photo of his daughter. When she asked why they couldn't see it right away, the inventor devised the Model 95 Polaroid Land camera, the first camera to develop pictures on the spot. He was born in Connecticut, but attended Harvard University, and his company was located in Cambridge.

Kathryn Lasky (?–) is an author who has gained critical acclaim for her work, including the Dear America series and the Guardians of Ga'Hoole series. She was born in Indiana, but now lives in Cambridge.

Lewis Latimer (1848–1928) improved on Thomas Edison's lightbulb and designed one with a filament that lasted longer than a few days. This was a huge breakthrough in lighting that made electric lights practical for use in homes and along streets. He was born in Chelsea.

Jay Leno (1950–) is a comedian best known for hosting *The Tonight Show with Jay Leno*. He was born in New York, but was raised in Andover and graduated from Emerson College in Boston.

Henry Wadsworth Longfellow (1807–1882) was a poet, noted for *The Song of Hiawatha* and *Paul Revere's Ride*. Born in Maine, he was educated at Bowdoin and later became a professor at Harvard.

Francis Cabot Lowell (1775–1817) was fascinated by a power loom he saw during a trip to Great Britain. Upon his return, he and his partner, Paul Moody, built and improved a power loom. This invention changed the face of U.S. industry. Lowell was born in Newburyport.

Horace Mann See page 70.

Rocky Marciano (1923–1969) was a boxer who was heavyweight champion of the world from 1952 to 1956. He was born in Brockton.

Donald McKay (1810–1880) was a master shipbuilder who designed some of the largest, longest, and fastest clipper ships in the world. In the 1850s, McKay's *Flying Cloud* set speed records that have yet to be broken. He was born in Nova Scotia, but moved to Newburyport and later East Boston.

Metacom, Metacomet, or **King Philip (c.1639–1676)** was a sachem of the Wampanoag tribe who led an unsuccessful tribal revolt against the colonists, called King Philip's War.

Samuel Morse (1791–1872) was a professional painter who invented the electronic telegraph. He came up with a special code, now called Morse code, to use with his machine. He was born in Charlestown.

Jay Leno

Nanapashemet See page 27.

Leonard Nimoy (1931–) is an actor best known for starring as Mr. Spock in *Star Trek*. He was born and raised in Boston.

Conan O'Brien (1963–) is a comedian best known for hosting *Late Night with Conan O'Brien*. He was born in Brookline and graduated from Harvard University.

Seiji Ozawa (1935–) was born in Japan and attended the Tanglewood Music Center in the Berkshires. In 1973, he became the conductor of the Boston Symphony Orchestra and remained in that position for 29 years.

Deval Patrick (1956–) became the first African American governor of Massachusetts when he was elected in November 2006.

Charles Lenox Redmond (1810–1878) and **Sarah Parker Redmond (1826–1894)** were siblings born to free black parents. They were noted abolitionists who traveled the world speaking out about slavery.

Paul Revere (1735–1818) was a Boston silversmith, engraver, and patriot.

Norman Rockwell (1894–1978) was an artist well known for illustrating covers for the *Saturday Evening Post*. He lived in Stockbridge.

Seiji Ozawa

Lucy Stone

Deborah Sampson (1760–1827) was 21 years old when she disguised herself as a man and joined the 4th Massachusetts Regiment during the American Revolution. When she was injured, her secret was out. But she was the first American woman to see combat and the first female to earn a U.S. military pension. She was born in Plymouth County.

Lucy Stone (1818–1893) grew up in West Brookfield. She put herself through Oberlin College in Ohio and became the first woman in Massachusetts to earn a college diploma.

Tisquantum See page 32.

Henry David Thoreau See page 15.

Mark Wahlberg (1971–) is an acclaimed actor and producer, once known as rap artist Marky Mark. He was born in Dorchester.

Daniel Webster (1782–1852) was a Boston senator known for his powerful speeches.

Phillis Wheatley See page 39.

Eli Whitney (1765–1825) was the inventor of the cotton gin. He was born in Westborough.

Ted Williams See page 74.

John Winthrop (1588–1649) was the first governor of Massachusetts Bay Colony.

RESOURCES

BOOKS

Nonfiction

Bjorklund, Ruth. *Massachusetts*. Tarrytown, N.Y.: Benchmark Books, 2002.

DeAngelis, Gina. *The Massachusetts 54th: African American Soldiers of the Union*. Mankato, Minn.: Bridgestone Books, 2002.

Dolan, Edward F. *The Boston Tea Party*. Tarrytown, N.Y.: Benchmark Books, 2001.

Douglass, Frederick. *Escape from Slavery: The Boyhood of Frederick Douglass in His Own Words*. New York: Knopf Books for Young Readers, 1993.

Gellerman, Brian, and Erik Sherman. *Massachusetts Curiosities: Quirky Characters, Roadside Oddities, and Other Offbeat Stuff*. Guilford, Conn.: The Globe Pequot Press, 2004.

Irvin, Benjamin H. *Samuel Adams: Son of Liberty, Father of Revolution*. New York: Oxford University Press, 2002.

Levy, Janey. *The Wampanoag of Massachusetts and Rhode Island*. New York: Rosen Publishing Group, 2005.

Riehecky, Janet. *The Wampanoag: The People of the First Light*. Mankato, Minn.: Bridgestone Books, 2003.

Weidt, Maryann N. *Fighting for Equal Rights: A Story About Susan B. Anthony*. Minneapolis: Lerner Publishing Group, 2003.

Yolen, Jane, and Heidi Elisabet Y. Stemple. *The Salem Witch Trials: An Unsolved Mystery from History*. New York: Simon and Schuster Children's Publishing, 2004.

Fiction

Alcott, Lousia May. *Little Women*. New York: Signet Classics, 2004.

Forbes, Esther. *Johnny Tremain*. New York: Yearling, 1980 reissue.

Johnson, Angela. *Looking for Red*. New York: Simon & Schuster Children's Publishing, 2002.

Kohler, Jackie French. *Someday*. New York: Orchard, 2002.

Murphy, T. M. *The Secrets of Belltown*. Exeter, N.H.: J. N. Townsend Publishing, 2001.

Voight, Cynthia. *The Callendar Papers*. New York: Aladdin, 2000.

DVDs

American Experience: The Massachusetts 54th Colored Infantry. PBS Home Video, 2005.
Benjamin Franklin. PBS Home Video, 2002.
Biography: Frederick Douglass. A&E DVD Archives, 2005.
Cape Cod National Seashore. Finley-Holiday Film Corp, 2005.
Discover America: Massachusetts. Bennett-Watt Media, 2006.
JFK: A Presidency Revealed. The History Channel, 2003.

WEB SITES AND ORGANIZATIONS

Boston Children's Museum
300 Congress Street
Boston, MA 02210
617/426-8855
www.bostonchildrensmuseum.org/educators/
wampanoag.html
Explore the history of the Wampanoag
people through the powerful words of tribal
members past and present.

Greater Boston Convention and Visitors Bureau
Two Copley Place, Suite 105
Boston, MA 02116-6501
888/SEE BOSTON
www.bostonusa.com
Log on to this site to learn more about sports,
music, dining, and shopping in Boston. Get
up-to-date tourism facts and statistics.

Massachusetts Foundation for the Humanities
101 Walnut Street
Watertown, MA 02472
617/923-1678
www.massmoments.org
This is an excellent Web site that features audio
and visual stories covering Massachusetts's
most important historical happenings.

Massachusetts Office of Travel & Tourism
10 Park Plaza, Suite 4510
Boston, MA 02116
800/227-MASS
www.mass-vacation.com
Practically everything there is to see and do
in Massachusetts can be found here. Log on
to find museums, roadside hotspots, tourist
attractions, fairs, festivals, concerts, events,
and regional activities across the Bay State.

Plimoth Plantation
137 Warren Avenue
Plymouth, MA 02360
508/746-1622
www.plimoth.org
Explore the "living museum" of Plimoth
Plantation at this Web site.

Secretary of the Commonwealth
McCormack Building
One Ashburton Place, Room 1611
Boston, MA 02108-1512
617/727-7030
www.sec.state.ma.us/cis/cisidx.htm
This site has tons of facts, figures, maps, and
trivia about Massachusetts's cities, people,
and government.

INDEX

★ ★ ★

AUTHOR'S TIPS AND SOURCE NOTES

★ ★ ★

Anyone who has seen the splendor of the Berkshires in the fall knows you may leave Massachusetts, but it never leaves you. Magically, it keeps calling you back. In researching *Massachusetts*, I drew on my own wonderful experiences traveling throughout New England over the past 20 years, as well as interviews with the vibrant people who live, work, and play in the Bay State. I'm a former television news reporter, so asking questions comes almost as naturally as breathing! Books, newspaper articles, DVDs, videos, and Internet sites helped round out my research. More than 150 sources were tapped for this book, but I'll just mention a few here.

Books such as William Bradford's *Of Plymouth Plantation: 1620–1647,* Frederick Douglass's *My Bondage and My Freedom,* and David Silverman's *Faith and Boundaries: Colonists, Christianity, and Community Among the Wampanoag Indians of Martha's Vineyard, 1600–1871* gave the dynamic firsthand accounts every history writer searches for.

I looked to the Internet for more about specific topics, such as the Cape Cod National Seashore (*www.nps.gov/caco*), the Quabbin Reservoir (*www.foquabbin. org*), and the Berkshires (The Nature Conservancy has a great site devoted to this stunning region: *www.lastgreatplaces.org/berkshire/index.html*).

Phone and e-mail interviews allowed me to gather in-depth details, up-to-date statistics, and personal viewpoints. I am grateful to those who shared their passion for the Bay State with me, among them Bob Guillemin, Joan Lederman, Keith Lincoln, and Binh Phu. Special thanks to Bill DeSousa at the Cape Cod Chamber of Commerce, who so graciously provided me with information and resources at every turn. Thanks also to the Massachusetts Office of Travel & Tourism, the Boston Public Library, and the Boston Historical Society.